50 Climbs (By Bike) in Utah

A guide to cycling climbing and the state's greatest hill climbs

Help Keep This Guide Up to Date

Diligence was put forth by the author to provide as accurate as possible the information contained in this guide. However, things change over time (roads close, starting and/or points are re-routed, etc.).

If you encounter alternate conditions from those stated here or have additional climbs to include and/or suggestions for improvement please send those to:

extreme.press@yahoo.com

Other climbing guides by the author include:

The Complete Guide to Climbing By Bike (2nd Edition)
The Complete Guide to Climbing By Bike in California (2nd Edition)
The Complete Guide to Climbing By Bike in Colorado
The Complete Guide to Climbing By Bike in the Southeast

Information on these guides can be found at the website: **www.usacyclingclimbing.com**

Complete Guide to Climbing by Bike Series

50 Climbs (By Bike) in Utah

A guide to cycling climbing and the state's greatest hill climbs

John Summerson

Extreme Press
405 Kettle Court
Winston-Salem, NC 27104
336 659-7600
Extreme.press@yahoo.com

An Extreme Press Guide

June, 2014

All photos by the author except for Squaw Peak (Michael Kelsey)

Library of Congress Control Number: 2014932517

ISBN 13: 978-0-9792571-5-5

"The best climbers do not suffer less; they just suffer faster" - Chris Boardman

Front cover - The east side of Alpine Summit
Back cover - Along Empire Pass near Park City

Table of Contents

Preface 9
Introduction 11
Climbing 12
About this Guidebook 17
Definitions of Terms 19
Hitting the Road 22
Improving Climbing Ability 25
Cycling Techniques 25
Specific Training for Hill Climbing 28
Descending 39
Mental Training 40

Northern Utah

1. Bear Lake Summit East 46
2. Bear Lake Summit West 48
3. North Ogden Divide East 50
4. North Ogden Divide West 52
5. Powder Mountain 54
6. Monte Cristo Summit East 58
7. Monte Cristo Summit West 60
8. Snow Basin Road 62
9. Trappers Loop North 64

10. Bald Mountain Pass West 66
11. Wolf Creek Summit East....68
12. Wolf Creek Summit West....70
13. 44 North....72
14. 191 North....74
15. 191 South....76

Salt Lake City/Provo/Midway

16. City Creek Canyon 80
17. Emigration Canyon....82
18. East Canyon 84
19. Big Mountain....86
20. Millcreek Canyon....88
21. Big Cottonwood Canyon....90
22. Little Cottonwood Canyon 92
23. Traverse Ridge Road....94
24. Suncrest Drive 96
25. Alpine Summit East 98
26. Alpine Summit West 100
27. Squaw Peak 102
28. Guardsman Pass East....104
29. Empire Pass North 108
30. Empire Pass South....110
31. Snake Creek Road 112

Central Utah

32. Nebo Loop Road North 116
33. Nebo Loop Road South 118
34. Indian Canyon South 120
35. 264 East 122
36. 31 East 124
37. 31 West 126

Southern Utah

38. 153/Eagle Point 130
39. Fremont Pass West 132
40. Boulder Mountain North 134
41. Boulder Mountain South 136
42. Castle Valley 138
43. The Big Nasty 140
44. 143 North 142
45. 143 East 144
46. Cedar Canyon 146
47. Right Hand Canyon 148
48. Kolob Canyon 150
49. Kolob Reservoir Road 152
50. Zion National Park 154

Other Climbs

Trappers Loop South 156
Bald Mountain Pass North 156
32 West 157
Hobble Creek Right Fork 157
Fremont Pass East 158
Red Canyon 158
Bryce Canyon West 159
12 West 159
Escalante East and West 160
Castle Valley/Gateway 161
Arches National Park 161
Canyonlands National Park 162
Snow Canyon 162

Most Difficult Climbs 163
Climbing Categories
- Greatest Elevation Gain Climbs 166
- Highest Elevation Attained Climbs 166
- Longest Climbs 167
- Steepest Climbs 167
- Fastest Descents 168
- Most Scenic Climbs 168

Additional Data 170
Climb Logs 189

Preface

Once one visits Utah it quickly becomes apparent that it is a special place. The outstanding scenery and unique topography are quite well known to many. What may not be as well known are its generous paved climbs as the state contains a wide variety including some of the most difficult and spectacular in the United States. From low desert sandstone lined defiles to high altitude alpine ascents, there is something here for everyone who enjoys an uphill challenge. And while there are many reasons to climb a hill on a bicycle, it may be best not to wonder why but to simply enjoy the experience, whatever the end results may be.

The people of Utah are a hardy bunch and that includes their numerous cyclists, many of whom relish a challenge; one that their state gladly serves up. While the data collection for this guide involved quite a bit of effort and time, I can honestly state that I thoroughly enjoyed every minute of it, spanning the state from Bear Lake Summit to Castle Valley; from Park City to St George. While slot canyons initially drew me to this place, it is cycling and its climbs that keep me coming back.

Introduction

Road bike cycling is one of the most popular sports in the world and the biggest challenge within the sport, and its most intriguing aspect, is hill climbing. Major professional cycling tours such as the Tour de France are usually won and lost in the mountains. But why climb the hill?

Climbing is also the most difficult part of cycling, requiring great energy and effort and on tough hills or going all out, producing discomfort or even pain. Why, then, do cyclists routinely engage in a painful activity that can result, as they themselves describe, in great suffering for the sole purpose of reaching the top? In the case of professional riders it could be argued that they are paid to do it. For others, answers may include losing weight or improving one's racing ability or fitness level. But I think the real answer is because it's there. This simple phrase sums up the main reason people undertake physical challenges. Be it mountain climbing, distance running or peak-bagging by bike, the main reason cyclists will tolerate the pain is for the physical and mental challenge itself. Hills are there to be beaten.

For years, major cycling events such as the Tour

de France have evoked the image of the lone rider struggling up sheer alpine pitches, straining their physical limits. Cycling greats such as Eddy Merckx, Bernard Hinault and Lance Armstrong, while very complete all-around riders, became legends in the sport in large part from their climbing exploits. The mountains add an almost mythic quality to races as the riders are seen overcoming obstacles that extend beyond the actual asphalt, rock and dirt upon which they climb. Average cyclists also feel the allure of attempting difficult climbs and achieve tremendous satisfaction from a successful summit. It sounds pretty simple. Find a mountain with a paved road to the top and then pedal up it. However, hill climbing is not easy, as certain climbs involve ascents of thousands of vertical feet. Elite riders can race to the top but success for most involves just getting there.

Climbing

No one may know when the first significant hill was climbed on a bicycle but the first documentation of major ascents occurred in professional stage races which originated in Europe, the oldest being the Tour de France (first held in 1903). It is interesting to note that the first two Tours did not include any mountain

SUMMIT
7600 FT.

passes. Bikes were heavy, single speed (and brake) behemoths while many roads were unpaved. Some felt that the riders of the day could not complete big climbs and that adding them to the race route would ruin the Tour. It was not until 1905 that significant climbs were added, the very first being the Ballon d'Alsace in the Vosges Mountains. In 1910 the first major, high altitude passes were added (four major climbs in the Pyrenees Mountains including the now famous Tourmalet) which resulted in a great deal of criticism directed at race organizers that the routes were too difficult. As is often the case human potential was underestimated as many riders of that era conquered the climbs in dramatic fashion.

In contrast, 1910 was also the year that the broom wagon was introduced to sweep riders up who could not finish the stage. In 1911 the first major climb in the Alps was added (Col de Galibier) with spectacular results. Instead of being a detriment, the uphill duels captured the public imagination and added to the popularity of the event. The race route every year thereafter has contained many significant climbs. Other major tours that followed also began to include hills along their routes. In 1933 the Tour de France and the Giro d'Italia (Italy's national tour) began recognizing the best climbers in the field (Spain's Vicente Trueba was the first winner in the Tour along with Alfredo Binda in the Giro). Most of the major stage races now recognize this accomplishment as the cyclists earn points based upon their finish in a climb and its difficulty. The cyclist with the most accumulated points is awarded the Polka Dot Jersey as the winner of the king of the mountains competition.

The performances of great early climbers such as Alfredo Binda, Fausto Coppi and Charley Gaul continued to increase the popularity of the major tours. These events made climbs such as the Tourmalet and L'Alpe d'Huez in France and Stelvio in Italy as well known to cycling fans as the Daytona Speedway or Yankee Stadium are to U.S. racing and baseball fans, respectively. The mountains allowed bike races to become truly great as the event rose beyond the personal concerns of the cyclists to reflect life as a whole.

Today hill climbing is more popular than ever and within multi-stage races those with hilltop finishes are usually the most anticipated and best attended stages of the race. Fans realize that hills offer the best opportunity to view the drama within the peloton as it struggles through the most difficult and important element in any race. Cyclists know that making it to the top of a solid hill can be quite satisfying and used as a measure of fitness and/or progress. Climbing adds the mythic quality of overcoming obstacles that continues to be associated with the major cycling tours and which has produced many memorable moments. Ascending difficult hills is about struggle and perseverance and it is these aspects that have made conquering the mountains the heart and soul of cycling.

The steep Wasatch along the east side of Alpine Summit

About This Guidebook

Utah's mountainous terrain provides ample opportunities for uphill riding, as long as there is a paved road along the way. From the steep Wasatch and Uinta ranges in the north to the high plateaus and broken canyon country in the central and southern portions of the state, there are elevation challenging stretches of pavement in every direction and almost all of them also provide outstanding scenery. In fact, there are paved roads from 2,500 to over 10,000 feet of elevation here. As such the sport of cycling is growing in popularity.

While road bike cycling and hill climbing in particular are enjoying a surge in popularity, there is little published information on the location of the most difficult road bike hill climbs and very little accurate data on the length and elevation gain of these climbs. Many roads in Utah are hilly but that is not the intent of this guide. The location, description and profiling of notable individual hills is its aim. As such, I set out to publish a guide for those cyclists looking specifically for this information. There are hundreds of paved ascents within Utah so obviously they all cannot be included in these pages. What this guidebook does attempt to include are the most difficult road bike climbs in the state (see appendix for an attempt at climb rankings). Many other U.S. ascents can be found in the author's nationwide and regional climbing guides (currently the Southeast, California and Colorado).

You will notice that each climb in this guide is given a difficulty rating (5 levels) listed just below the climb name in its description. This is the same system that major cycling tours use to describe the difficulty of their included ascents. The most difficult are described as 'beyond category'. There are few of these monsters out there. The 2nd most difficult classification is Category 1. Category 2s are a bit less difficult and Category 3 and 4 follow as easier ascents, respectively. These are broad categories so there can be quite a difference in difficulty between two climbs described as category 1 for instance.

Beyond Category	- Most Difficult
Category 1	- Difficult
Category 2	- A Bit Less Difficult
Category 3	- A Bit Less Difficult Still
Category 4	- Least Difficult

Appendices in this guide rank Utah climbs by

overall difficulty (based on a numeric formula), average grade, summit elevation, elevation gain, and several other categories. While some of the hills in this guide are for the serious road cyclist only, there are many more moderate climbs for the rider looking to improve their climbing skills and/or fitness level. Be sure to know your fitness and ability level before you tackle the longer and/or more difficult hills in this book. Start with the shorter, less steep climbs and progress from there. As all are located in the mountains, the scenery along the way is usually spectacular and will help ease the pain of a tough ascent.

Several UT hills are out of bounds and thus not included in these pages. This includes excellent Lamb's Canyon near Salt Lake City with its private upper section; isolated and solid Oak City Canyon, currently closed due to fire induced danger and Wolf Creek Ranch east of Heber City, raced in the annual Tour of Utah but a private road. I also chose not to include hills with high speed traffic which left out Soldiers Summit along busy Route 6.

Definitions of Terms

This guide will use several terms to describe each

climb, which are defined below:

Total elevation - This is the elevation gained in feet from the starting point to the top of the climb. If a climb has descents within it this additional climbing is not included in the total elevation gained. Elevations were measured using global positioning satellite (GPS) positions from which a very accurate elevation was then determined by plotting the fixed point using a topographic software program.

Length - This is the distance of the climb in miles. If you are retracing your route back to the starting point, in order to determine the total distance of the ride, simply double the climb's length. Climb lengths were measured by automobile odometer (at least two measures and averaged) and cycle computer where applicable.

Average Grade (maximum grade) - This is the average percent grade or steepness of the climb and is expressed as a percentage (8%). The grade assigned to each hill is the average grade over the entire climb. The higher the percent grade, the steeper the climb. Percent grade is determined by dividing the elevation gain by the length of the climb.

The maximum grade is just that. The measured maximum must extend all the way across the road (a very steep inside corner that could be bypassed for instance does not qualify) and be at least a bike length in length. Maximum gradient was hand measured by gradiometer.

In the listed climb descriptions the distance and elevation data only reflect the contiguous portion of the road that is part of the climb. If the climb includes small flats or descents, they are included in the distance but do not contribute to the net elevation gain. Thus the average grade may not in some cases accurately represent the true nature of the climb. That is, there are usually sections on the climb that are steeper than the average grade along with sections that are less steep than the average grade.

Time - This is an estimate of the amount of time needed to complete each climb. It is listed through a fairly wide range in order to attempt to take into account individual fitness levels. Some extremely proficient riders could complete the hill under the listed time and a few may not be able to complete it within the upper time range.

Directions - The starting point for almost all

directions for climbs listed in this guidebook is the nearest city or town, some of which are very tiny places. A good road map will be helpful to locate and reach many of these locations which in turn begin the journey to the climbs start. I would recommend the Utah state map by Delorme but any reasonable national or state highway road map should get you where you need to go. Web based mapping software can also help you locate each ascent.

Hitting the Road

All of this said you have to get on the bike and hit the road in order to climb. Toward that end, the following are summaries of some cycling habits and wisdom to consider before you take on that big climb you have always wanted to summit. While it may be useful to review, cyclists can consider all or only a few of these items as needed.

Rules of the Road

- Follow the same driving rules as motorists and be sure to obey all traffic patterns
- Wear a helmet and bright colors so you are more visible

- Ride single file on particularly busy roads so that motorized vehicles can pass and use hand signals to alert motorists of your next move
- Ride with traffic and not against it and make eye contact with drivers and assume they do not see you
- Be particularly alert in foggy, rainy or windy conditions
- In summer ride early to high altitude to avoid thunder storms and down slope winds in the afternoon
- Give parked cars a wide berth and be alert for sewer grates, manhole covers, cattle guards, oil, gravel, wet leaves and ice
- Many listed climbs are fairly long rides by themselves so go prepared with extra tube along with pump, tool kit, rain gear, food and fluids
- It is usually best to ride with a partner or three. In case of emergency one rider can go for help if needed
- Some climbs in this guide are closed by snow in winter (noted in climb description). As the length of the season varies greatly at altitude, call ahead in late Spring and Fall for possible road closures

Pre-Ride Check

- Check tires for proper inflation, brakes for traction
- Check all quick releases to make sure they are tight
- Check the chain and all nuts and bolts for tightness.
- Spin your wheels through frame and brakes to make sure they are rolling true
- Make sure you have all necessary gear for the particular ride
- Bring a positive attitude along whenever possible

The top of Trappers Loop near Ogden

Improving Climbing Ability

For new cyclists, hill climbing is one of the most daunting aspects of riding. More experienced riders, however, enjoy climbing and regard tough hills as a challenge. It is a great feeling to make a solid climb and then enjoy the descent down the other side. The simplest way to improve your climbing technique and the best training for climbing is to climb; that is, to incorporate hills into your rides. However, don't start climbing big hills until you have built up an adequate cycling fitness base. Try to accumulate a significant amount of relatively flat riding first. At that point add shorter/moderate grade hills to your rides and work your way up to the longer and/or steeper climbs. Incorporating hills in your riding will not make them any shorter but eventually they may feel that way.

Cycling Techniques for Climbing

Improving your basic cycling techniques can also improve your climbing ability. It is important to maintain a smooth, steady rhythm as you pedal up the hill. Unless very short in length, start a climb with as slow a pace as possible. This will allow you to develop a rhythm which not only includes the pedaling cadence but breathing as well. Breathe slowly and deeply as this will help establish a smooth pedaling cadence. Obviously in your pedal stroke it is much easier to apply force to the pedals when your foot is on the down stroke. However, this results in uneven power output contributing to slight accelerations and decelerations of the bike which become exaggerated when climbing. To remedy this try to lift your knee and drag your foot backwards across the bottom of the pedal stroke, pulling upwards slightly on the upstroke and pulling the pedal forward across the top of its rotation.

There are several other factors to consider when climbing. First, make sure you have proper gearing. At least a 39-tooth small chain ring in front and a 25-tooth rear gear (a 27 or 28 rear or triple front rings are even better if you will be riding consistently on steep hills). Upon encountering a hill, do not shift too soon as this can result in a momentum loss from a high RPM spinning effect. Conversely, you must not end up in a gear that is too large which tends to tire one out. The proper climbing cadence varies among individuals. The idea with gearing is to maintain a cadence that is comfortable, shifting as you tire and the RPM's start to drop. Basically, if the gradient varies on the climb adjust your gearing so that your cadence and level of effort are maximized.

Another factor is whether to sit or stand during the ascent. Seated is more energy efficient but a standing position can produce much more power. A simple rule to start with is that if the hill is long, climb in the saddle, and if short or while attacking, stand. Reality dictates that on most challenging hills you will do both. For the majority of the climb most will find it is more efficient to sit in the saddle. Put your hands on the top of the brake hoods or handlebars and keep them relaxed. Try to change their positioning periodically. The upper body should not be crunched forward too far and the shoulders should be open. This will allow for easier breathing as the climb continues. Relax your upper body as well, as this will decrease oxygen demands.

Your weight should be over the cranks to maximize power during the pedal stroke. Try not to bounce on the pedals as you shift from side to side. Developing a rhythm that combines pedaling and breathing will make a big difference in your climbing efficiency. At times you will need to stand such as on very steep sections or when sprinting past a fellow rider. Just before you stand, shift to a higher gear as you can generate more power in this position (shift back when you sit down again). As you come off of the saddle continue with an even pedal stroke and push your hands forward. Come out of the saddle on the down stroke to minimize loss of momentum.

Specific Training for Hill Climbing

While the physiology of human performance training is much more understood today than in the past, training is still part art and science. That is, there is more than one way to improve performance. However, perhaps the more important considerations are time and commitment. Time to train is obviously limited for most. With that in mind it is paramount that this limited time is put to good use. Intensity is the key with adequate rest for recovery. Particularly with hill climbing which may involve very intense bursts of effort, adequate recovery is essential to avoid overtraining and burnout. In addition, train consistently for best results. Develop specific climbing goals and a plan to reach those goals. Listen to your body and back off if needed. Commit to climbing success and it will likely follow.

Good climbers have certain attributes that contribute to their success. All have an endurance base and have developed solid power to weight

6%
NEXT 1 MILE

ratios which gives the ability to generate greater amounts of force with each pedal stroke. They also tend to have high anaerobic endurance which results in greater levels of lactic acid tolerance. Training to improve climbing ability should focus on these physiologic aspects.

Build a Base

As previously mentioned make sure you have a solid cycling base before adding significant climbing to your riding and attempting the interval routines described later in this section. You should complete many miles of riding on mostly flat terrain to build your endurance base before moving on to more specialized routines for climbing. The amount of time needed will vary by individual, ranging from several months to several years of regular road cycling depending on age, health and fitness level. After a period of mainly flat riding, add moderate hills to your regular endurance rides. As you progress, add longer and steeper hills.

Power to Weight Ratio

Climbing ability has a strong correlation with power

to weight ratio; in fact it is perhaps the most accurate predictor of climbing success. As you may have noticed, the climbing specialists on the pro tour are almost all very lean (the late Marco Pantani particularly comes to mind). Thus, climbing can be improved by increasing power, losing body weight or, for the greatest results, a combination of the two.

Even a relatively small weight loss (3-5 lbs.) can produce significant improvement. How much might a bit of excess weight be costing you? It is estimated that one kilogram (2.2 lbs.) of excess fat on a moderate grade and at a fixed effort has a cost of ~3 seconds per kilometer. So 5 excess pounds on a 10 kilometer climb in theory can cost you over one minute. Much information is available regarding losing weight so this guide will not attempt to add to that body of knowledge. Just keep in mind that weight loss can lead to reductions in power output (to maintain power lose as much fat and as little muscle as possible). If you are serious about increasing your power output invest in a power meter and learn how to use it. A good reference is 'Training and Racing with a Power Meter' by Hunter Allen and Andrew Coggan. Increasing cycling power will be touched upon in the following sections and comes about through specific training.

Regarding the advantages of lower weight, do not forget your bike. As long as component stiffness is not compromised (stiffer rims and frames flex less during use and thus take less energy to push up hills) reducing your machine's weight will improve its ability to climb as well. Rotating weight is the real key so you will see the biggest gains from reductions in this area. Use the lightest rims, pedals and shoes you can afford. Tires with smoother and thinner treads and stronger sidewalls will also help.

Improving Lactate Threshold

Lactate threshold is the point at which lactic acid begins to accumulate above moderate levels, resulting in fatigue in the affected muscles. This quickly results in the inability to continue to perform at a level of work. Most riders know the heavy legged feeling after a hard push when you must slow down in order to keep going. The goal of lactate threshold training is to raise the point at which lactic acid accumulates in the muscles to the point to affect performance significantly. All things being equal, the higher your lactate threshold, the faster the pace you can hold on climbs.

While lactate threshold can be measured directly it correlates well with heart rate and is normally between 75-90% of maximum heart rate. The goal of climbing-specific training should be to increase that percentage towards the top of the range. A simple way to estimate your lactate threshold is to perform two bouts of work. When rested and motivated after a good warm-up, perform a twenty minute time trial at maximum effort and record your average heart rate. Repeat this test under similar conditions. The average heart rate for both efforts is a close approximation of your heart rate at your lactate threshold. Providing you have a sufficient aerobic endurance base (see 'Build a Base' above) lactate threshold training should improve your climbing ability. This is very demanding training however and will require proper recovery between bouts so don't forget to include easy days on the bike when needed.

Interval Routines

A very effective way to increase your power and to raise your lactate threshold in order to improve climbing ability is through the use of intervals. Intervals are relatively short bursts of more intense effort followed by a recovery period. Keep in mind that to fully benefit from these exercises your fitness level should be quite high before you incorporate them into your routine. Once fit, interval training may reduce the total amount of time you need to be on the bike as studies have typically shown equal improvements in power output between interval and longer duration aerobic training.

There are almost endless variations of interval exercises for those on the bike. Several of the below routines could be added (start at the top of the below list and progress down) to your regular riding training (1-3 times per week) depending upon the season and your fitness level. Typically use them more frequently for pre-season training; tapering off before races. Add/delete routines as needed. You could also make use of spinning classes at your local gym as well.

Recovery is a real key with intensive interval training so make sure you are fully (or almost fully) recovered between sets. This can be difficult to determine at times. Activity between intervals should be easy, high cadence spinning on mostly level ground if at all possible.

Big gear climbs - On various hill grades on your regular rides shift up one cog from normal (harder gear) for 1-2 minutes. Keep cadence at least 50 RPM and stay seated.

Cruise intervals - 3 to 5 intervals for 6-12 minutes each on a moderate grade (3-5%) at or just below your lactate threshold. Recover for 2-4 minutes. Gradually add minutes to each interval.

Anaerobic endurance intervals - 3-5 intervals for 2-4 minutes each on a 6-8% grade, gradually building the intensity, with cadence of at least 60 RPM. Intensity should be above your lactate threshold for the second half of the interval. Recovery should be double the interval length.

Extended Climbing at Lactate Threshold - On a steady and moderate grade, climb for 15-30 minutes at or just slightly above your lactate threshold. Gradually add minutes up to 30 (or the longest hill you may need to climb) for maximum effect.

Sit/Stand intervals - On a moderate hill and at a comfortable cadence, alternate seated and standing climbing of equal intervals. After thirty seconds in the saddle, stand on the pedals for 30 seconds. After another minute of climbing in the saddle, stand for one minute, etc. Gradually build the intervals up to 4-5 minutes each.

Hill Sprints - Perform 5-10 sprints for 10-15 seconds at maximum effort. Gradually move from moderate to steeper hills. Recover for five minutes between each sprint.

Hill Jumps - While climbing a moderate hill do 4-5 sets of 3-5 jumps for ten crank turns (both feet) at maximum effort. Recover for one minute between each jump and five minutes between each set.

Advanced Hill Jumps - On a moderate grade perform 3-5 two minute sets, attacking every thirty seconds for ten pedal strokes. Stand for the attacks which should be at maximum effort; stay seated otherwise. Recover for five minutes between sets.

Weight Training

One factor linked to climbing success is leg strength. Particularly if you cannot put in year round riding on hills, weight training sessions might be added to your weekly routine. Ideally hit the weight room 2-3 times per week in the off season and once per week in season if possible, tapering off before races or big rides. Increasing upper body strength also should not be ignored as it has the potential to reduce upper

BIKE
RACE
TUESDAY
EXPECT
DELAY

body fatigue and increasing lower body strength will give you the ability to push a bigger (harder) gear over the same hill.

While certainly not including all beneficial weight exercises, the following list of basic exercises may give you the most benefit for your time spent in the gym. Use your own judgment and seek out a professional for advice as needed.

Squat	- 2-3 sets of 8-12 repetitions
Leg press	- 2-3 sets of 8-12 repetitions
Calf raise	- 2-3 sets of 8-12 repetitions
Step-ups	- 2-3 sets of 8-12 repetitions
Bench press	- 2-3 sets of 8-12 repetitions
Lat pulldown	- 2-3 sets of 8-12 repetitions
Push-ups	- 2-3 sets of 25 repetitions
Sit-ups (crunches)	- 2-3 sets of 25 repetitions
Back extensions	- 2-3 sets of 25 repetitions

Descending

Descending ability, like most skills, is best obtained and improved with practice. The more time you can spend on descending, the more confidence and speed you will be able to develop. The most important aspect of descending is relaxation. Anxiety can narrow your concentration and you may miss a dangerous aspect of the road ahead. Speed is obviously important but pushing your speed to the point of fear will not help your descending skills. Work on relaxation and speed should follow. Keep a slight bend in the arms and slide back in the saddle, keeping your hands on the bar drops. One important riding habit to develop is to look far enough in front of you to match your descending pace. During a faster descent you need to watch the road much further in front of the bike. Set up well in advance of a curve and do whatever braking needs to done before entering the turn. If you are riding in a group, spread out. This will allow each rider to take their preferred line through the corners; critical in that you may not have time to adjust once you commit. It also allows a greater margin if a rider needs to brake.

For long descents you should use both brakes equally. Once in a turn any traction used for braking significantly reduces the traction available for cornering. In wet conditions the distance required to stop is extended. Lightly apply the brakes periodically on a wet descent to remove excess water from the rims. Compete only against yourself on a fast descent and exercise caution on unfamiliar roads by always being prepared for road debris or traffic around every blind corner. In many cases descents are followed by another climb; if so, try to spin the pedals as you approach the bottom so that you will be warmed up for the next section of riding. Take it easy, relax, concentrate on the road, and most importantly, practice descending, and you will find your skills improving.

Mental Training

As professional cyclist Chris Boardman once said "The best climbers do not suffer less, they just suffer faster". Climbing can be painful, suffering the name of the game at times. That said there may also be some less conventional ways to improve your climbing ability. Developing mental focus to enable one to block out distractions, including physical discomfort, is another attribute of good climbers. All negative thoughts must go during your ride. The minute you think you cannot make a climb is when you may get into trouble. Many riders are dropped on climbs before they reach their physical breaking point simply because of negative thoughts.

Begin working on mental focus by clearing your mind entirely. This can be a difficult skill to master but can be developed in stretches during long rides. Be patient as it sometimes takes time to see progress. Once this skill is developed begin to think of a single thought or image. Try to keep this single thought or image in your mind for extended periods. Once you have developed this ability you will find it much easier to concentrate over a climb. Work on visualizing images of light or soaring objects as you work your way up the hill. These images can lower the perception of effort. Even if climbing times are similar the effect should be one of additional energy for the remainder of the race or ride. Remember, everyone suffers on a tough climb. Climbing can be as much a mental as physical challenge, so try not to let a lack of self-confidence affect your performance. Developing ways to deal mentally with the physical aspects of getting over tough hills should produce better results on the road.

Summary

To get the most out of the time on your bike and to avoid overtraining refer to the below summary:

- Build a strong aerobic base before adding a lot of climbing mileage
- Add climbing to your regular training rides
- Utilize interval training to improve climbing ability
- Build up the intensity of your training slowly
- Train consistently for best results
- Eat a balanced diet
- Try to get a minimum of eight hours sleep every night
- Set short, medium and long-term goals
- Use a training diary and review when needed
- Consider a power meter for climbing (more advanced) training
- Keep proper perspective of your cycling
- Know yourself and adjust your workouts accordingly

- Don't forget to include easy days on the bike
- Use mental techniques to develop positive thoughts during climbing
- Practice descending skills to round out your mountain training

A tight switchback on Route 143 North

Climb Locations

This guide is divided into 4 regions; North, Central, South and the Salt Lake/Provo/Midway area. The general locations of the climbs listed are shown within the maps of the appropriate section of Utah that precede each of those sections. The numbers on each map contained within the white background ovals correspond to the climb's listing in the Table of Contents of this guide. Each hill's location is also described within their individual listing. A more precise graphic location can be determined through Google Maps or other web based mapping programs as needed.

Table of Contents listing - (1-5)

Northern Utah

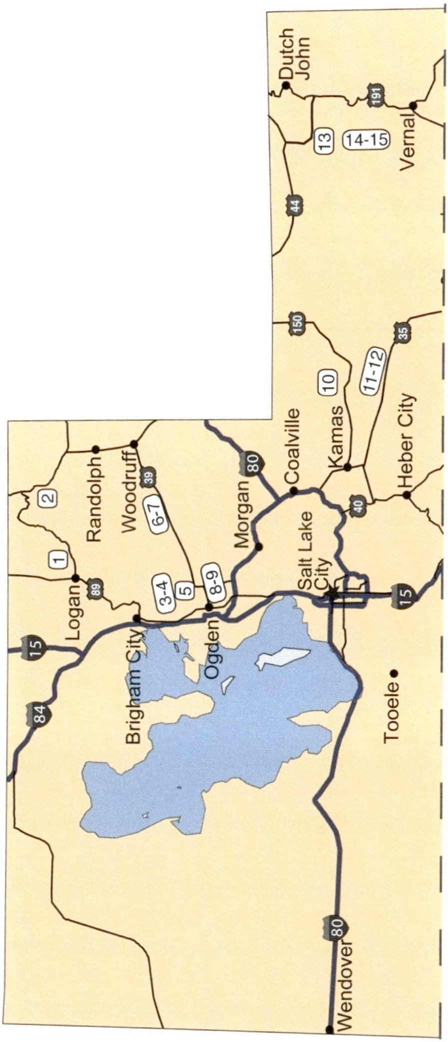

Bear Lake Summit East

Category 2

The east side of Bear Lake Summit is an interesting and medium length ascent located in the northeast corner of Utah. It offers views of isolated Bear Lake, one of the state's more spectacular attractions. Never steep, the grade is mostly steady and solid however and you may work to get to its summit. There is typically some intermittent traffic making the drive back and forth from Garden City and the lake to Logan but usually not enough to ruin the ride.

Over more shallow grade to begin, the slope soon pops up to its average as you gain altitude. The road swings up the mountain through multiple wide switchbacks which gives this hill an alpine feel. Once you leave the small town of Garden City there are a few interesting mountain houses along the way with big views of the lake below. Towards the top woods close in a bit and there are two lanes heading uphill for a bit more room. Moderate pedaling continues and the climb ends in a pleasant setting at an unmarked but obvious top at over 9,000 feet of elevation. There is a small parking area at the summit. The descent of the east side of Bear Lake Summit is a fun one as its grade produces some speed and the sweeping wide turns create a bit of a challenge in places.

Climb Stats:

Total elevation - 1,757 ft | **Length - 5.5 miles**

Average Grade - 6.1% (8%) | **Time - 30-60 minutes**

Directions - From tiny Garden City on scenic Bear Lake in the northeast corner of the state, head west on Route 89 where it makes a 90 degree turn to the west for 0.9 miles to begin the listed climb (right after the road bends to the left).

8%

Bear Lake Summit West

Category 2

The west side of Bear Lake Summit is a long and sinuous climb from Logan that reaches high altitude. The grade is quite shallow over most of its length but the hill does contain increased slope over the last few miles. Scenery is the real draw on this one as you will encounter quite different views over the lower compared to the upper section.

The road begins as twisty and over shallow grade as you follow the drainage up the mountain. There are quite a few items of interest along the way over its lower slopes (as well as a few small descents) so expect a bit a traffic moving about on some days. As you gain altitude the route straightens and you find a ramp or two of steeper pedaling but you will not encounter steep grade on this hill at any point. Increased tree cover is found along the way as well as thinning traffic as the miles tick by. At mile 25.5 the canyon widens with different views. You should be able to tell you have gained considerable altitude as well with the different scenery. Soon the grade increases for the steepest sustained climbing on the hill but the end is in sight. The summit is obvious so enjoy the views at the top if at all possible. The descent of Bear Lake Summit West is a long one and mostly uncomplicated except for perhaps needing to pay extra attention on the lower slopes due to its many twists, turns and turnouts.

Climb Stats:

Total elevation - 3,121 ft	**Length - 30.5 miles**
Average Grade - 1.9% (8%)	**Time - 90-150 minutes**

Directions - From the junction of Routes 89 and 91 in Logan, UT, head east on 89 for several miles to the bridge over the Logan River to begin by continuing east on 89.

North Ogden Divide East

Category 2

If you are looking for a true vertical challenge over a short course, the east side of North Ogden Divide can certainly deliver as it is one of the steepest climbs in Utah. These types of climbs seem to bludgeon you right from the start and this hill is no exception. There is a bit of traffic to accompany you at times but not enough to ruin the ride and the route does offer interesting views in places on the way up.

The grade is solid to start and gradually steepens as you ride west out of the scenic valley. Just beyond the initial half mile, the road makes a left hand turn and you quickly find yourself on double digit slope which remains with you for the majority of the rest of the ascent. There are views of the valley and mountains to your left here as well but keep your eyes on the road as it is quite narrow as it clings to the ridgeline with barriers in place (as of late 2013) which reduces your space to ride a bit further. The road gradually curves to the west as you continue to gain altitude through the divide. The grade eases just a bit as you near the summit which is unmarked but obvious. There is parking at the top (North Ogden Divide Trailhead) and the descent of this hill is a quick one so make sure you are ready for the right hand bend near the bottom.

Climb Stats:

Total elevation - 996 ft | **Length - 2.0 miles**

Average Grade - 9.4% (13%) | **Time - 12-25 minutes**

Directions - From Eden located east of Ogden, head north on Route 162 for several miles to its dead end at E 4100 N. Turn left (west) here and travel 0.9 miles to begin the climb where the grade changes significantly by continuing west.

25
MPH.

North Ogden Divide West

Category 2

The opposite side of North Ogden Divide is also a very steep test east of Ogden. It carries essentially the same average grade but for a longer distance, thus it is a significantly more difficult overall climb. Similar to the east side, the west side carries fairly steady traffic at times up its slopes but it is still a quite worthy ascent. One difference between the two is that views on the way up here are of the city of Ogden and the salt flats beyond instead of bucolic valley scenes.

The grade is solid to start and gradually steepens as you ride east out of a city neighborhood. The steep stuff arrives even earlier compared to the east side as the road curves towards the south so make sure you are warmed up. You again find double digit grade for the majority of the remainder of the climb but at least it is fairly steady so hopefully you can settle into some sort of rhythm. As mentioned, there are views of the city of Ogden for a time until the roadway bends back to the east, still over harsh slope. For the rest of the ascent you will ride between craggy mountain slopes with nothing in front of you except the summit, somewhere in the distance. Towards the very top the grade eases a bit and the top is reached at the North Ogden Divide Trailhead parking area.

Climb Stats:

Total elevation - 1,425 ft | **Length - 2.9 miles**

Average Grade - 9.3% (12%) | **Time - 15-30 minutes**

Directions - In Ogden, head east on E 3100 N to its junction with N 1150 E in the northeast corner of the city to begin the climb by continuing east (E 3100 N eventually becomes North Ogden Canyon Road).

Powder Mountain

Beyond Category

One of the most difficult overall climbs and the most difficult finish in Utah and perhaps the United States, Powder Mountain will slam you along long stretches of double digit grade in places along its route. Leading to a ski area, the road carries little traffic most days. It is a tale of two climbs in a sense with a relatively mild first half but a very challenging 2nd half so make sure you are prepared for this one. Initially it carries riders through a neighborhood and then into a rocky canyon within a national forest before ending among mountain homes.

From its start in a beautiful valley just north of the small town of Eden, the road heads toward the summit initially through a quiet neighborhood and past the Wolf Creek Resort along mostly moderate grade that includes a short flat section. There may be a few vehicles on this stretch which tend to disappear the higher you climb. The jagged peaks of the always impressive Wasatch Mountains surround you as you head higher. The residences thin as you continue east and once you leave the houses behind the grade rears up to double digit for a short distance, signaling danger ahead. The slope then eases just a bit as you head into national forest land with a somewhat more isolated feel to the ride. Slowly gaining altitude, soon more difficult pedaling returns however.

At mile 2.6 you pass through a small national forest gate and your pleasant ride is over for the day as it is here that the true nature of Powder Mountain is revealed. The next 3 miles average over 13% and include what is likely the steepest mile in Utah and one of the steepest in the United States. Just beyond the gate the grade hits 12-15% for extended stretches. This section is within a steep and rocky canyon as well which seems to add to its difficulty as there seems to be no way out except to keep moving forward up the hill. After a mile of super steep climbing the grade eases but only slightly as the road gently twists uphill through

16%

the rocky drainage. A bit higher up the cruel mountain road, a left hand bend carries you toward the ski area as the double digit torture continues. As a few signs of civilization appear the slope finally eases but only slightly. The 3 miles from the gate to this point may be the most difficult section of American climbing of that length west of Mount Washington in New Hampshire. At the small ski area the road makes a sharp turn to the right to reveal a few impressive mountain homes and the ascent ends soon after where the pavement ends at a large gravel parking area with scenic views to the east. While there is a bit of development on top, the prevailing feel is alpine (a fox was the only one on hand to watch the author crest this hill on a cool late May day). When you make it to the summit of this very difficult hill climb make sure to enjoy it and the surroundings as you will certainly have earned it.

Powder Mountain is similar to the Angliru in Spain and Mortirolo in Italy; two famous climbs used regularly in the Vuelta and Giro d'Italia, the national professional races of Italy and Spain respectively. As mentioned, it is one of the most difficult American climbs and includes what may be the most difficult finishing stretch of any U.S. hill so make sure you have some miles under your belt before you tackle this one. Due to its steep grade and fairly straight routing the descent is a wild one (very fast and has taken lives). Little traffic most days encourages high speed so keep your head going down.

Climb Stats:

Total elevation - 3,179 ft | **Length - 6.0 miles**

Average Grade - 10.0% (17%) | **Time - 45-90 minutes**

Directions - From Eden, UT east of Ogden head north on Route 162 for a short distance to a 4 way stop (Routes 162 and 158). From that junction head east on Route 158 (towards Wolf Creek Resort) for 1.2 miles to Willowbrook Lane (left) to begin the listed climb by continuing east.

AVALANCHE
DANGER
NEXT
3 MILES

Monte Cristo Summit East

Category 2

Do you prefer your hills long and lean? If so, the east side of Monte Cristo Summit certainly fits the bill as it is a lengthy and shallow grade climb located east of Ogden. This is ranching territory and the isolated setting guarantees little traffic for your summit attempt. You will ride within a shallow canyon over the lower part of the ascent but end up in a high mountain meadow with a true alpine feel among some of the largest stands of aspens in the state.

As mentioned you begin over shallow grade and within a drainage which gradually widens as you slowly gain altitude. The road tends to get a bit steeper the further west you go but it is never steep on this long hill. After approximately 4 miles of riding you will cross a cattle guard as the road begins to get a bit more twisty. Eventually you break out into a wide valley as the route begins to move uphill through wide curves and over moderate and steady overall grade. Stands of big pines and aspens begin to appear as you climb higher but keep in mind almost the entire ride is exposed to the sun. Towards the very top the grade eases and the listed top is reached (unmarked) just beyond the Monte Cristo campgrounds. The top of its listed west side (next climb) is 4.2 miles further west.

Climb Stats:

Total elevation - 2,490 ft **Length - 18.5 miles**

Average Grade - 2.6% (7%) **Time - 75-140 minutes**

Directions - In the small town of Woodruff, UT at the junction of Routes 89 and 39, head east on 39 for 1.6 miles to begin the climb (unmarked start - look for the grade increase) by continuing west up the hill.

Monte Cristo Summit West

Category 1

The west side of Monte Cristo Summit is another long and steady grade climb to quite high altitude that begins in a somewhat isolated setting east of the small town of Huntsville. More difficult overall than its east side (a bit shorter but steeper overall), the route rarely carries traffic and any you find thins considerably the higher you climb. Don't let its low average grade fool you however as it is a category 1 rated climb and can work you up to its high altitude top.

This one begins by heading east on Route 39 over shallow grade. The slope tends to gradually increase as you ride but never gets steep on this hill. Beginning within a drainage and among a few residences here and there, eventually the road breaks out to reveal a more alpine setting. The wider valley you then find yourself in is filled with pines and some of the largest aspen groves anywhere. The route eventually flows through some wide curves as you ride along a variably steady grade up the hill. Towards the very top long views of the surrounding mountains are revealed. The grade then eases up to its unmarked summit (0.5 miles beyond the Cache County line). Beyond, the roadway continues to climb intermittently and very shallowly for a short distance.

Climb Stats:

Total elevation - 3,480 ft	**Length - 16.2 miles**
Average Grade - 4.1% (8%)	**Time - 75-150 minutes**

Directions - From the junction of Routes 166 and 39 in the small village of Huntsville, UT, head east on 39 for 8.2 shallow grade miles to Causey Road on the right to begin the listed climb by continuing east on 39.

Snowbasin Road

Category 2

The old road up to the Snowbasin ski area, while not a particularly difficult climb, is a very pleasant route along a twisty and narrow roadway. Never steep, the pavement does contain some solid ramps along with one fairly long descent. It is a very scenic ascent that sees little traffic much of the time and has big mountain views in places.

The climb begins from Route 39 over solid grade as you enter a neighborhood. The route is quite twisty through this section as you generally ride southwest along the ridgeline of the foothills of the mountain with interesting views. Just under 3 miles in, the road undergoes a significant descent which lasts for just over one mile. Climbing then resumes over moderate grade as you leave the residences behind with massive Mount Ogden in front of you. Quickly you enter some trees over this section which has a more alpine feel and a twisty routing. At mile 7 you reach the Snowbasin ski area but keep heading uphill to the east to finish. This last section is over moderate slope and the road opens a bit toward the summit with good views of the surrounding mountains. Never steep, the length of Snowbasin Road will work you to its unmarked top (0.9 miles beyond the ski area) in a pleasant setting.

Climb Stats:

Total elevation - 1,627 ft | **Length - 7.9 miles**

Average Grade - 3.9% (8%) | **Time - 30-60 minutes**

Directions - From Ogden head east on Route 39 to the Pineview Reservoir and Snow Basin Road on the right (just before you reach Route 167) to begin the climb by heading up Snow Basin Road.

Trappers Loop North

Category 2

One of many hills in the area, the north side of Trappers Loop (Route 167) is a solid hill that does carry some vehicle traffic at times on part of its route. It finishes just short of the Snowbasin Ski Area in a dramatic setting. The climb carries a variable overall grade over most of its length and provides very long views of dramatic mountains.

The hill begins over stout but steady grade and in wide open surroundings. As mentioned there will likely be some traffic on this section but the road is 4 lane so there is plenty of room for riding. Settle into a grove here and keep pedaling and check out the long views in places. After several miles of solid climbing the slope eases. A mile later it eases dramatically and from here you now stair step up the ridge. Around 4 miles in, turn right suddenly towards the west and Mount Ogden. This final section is flat and then shallow early but quickly provides moderate grade climbing as you head west toward the ski area. Soon you encounter a descent. It is fairly short and climbing then resumes over again moderate grade. The listed top then suddenly appears as the road descends down to the Snowbasin ski area. The descent portion on Route 167 is quite fast. The south side of Trappers Loop is a less steep hill with views (5.3 miles in length at ~4% average grade).

Climb Stats:

Total elevation - 1,650 ft	**Length - 5.8 miles**
Average Grade - 5.4% (8%)	**Time - 20-40 minutes**

Directions - At the junction of Routes 39 and 167 east of Ogden and just south of Pineview Reservoir, the climb begins by heading north on 167 up the hill.

WATCH FOR
SNOWPLOWS
IN YOUR LANE

Bald Mountain Pass West

Category 1

The west side of Bald Mountain Pass is a very long and shallow climb to the highest elevation for a paved road in Utah. Over more solid grade towards the top, the start of the hill is quite shallow as you leave the town of Kamas and ride through long stretches of thick woods. The highlight of this one however may be its spectacular alpine scenery particularly evident above 10,000 feet of elevation.

As mentioned you begin over shallow grade as you head east toward the mountains. The slope is variable in places but you will never encounter steep pedaling. You pass an area of cabins several miles into the ascent and traffic is intermittent for the most part on this climb. Enjoy the scenery and keep pushing the pedals to the east through these pleasant surroundings for what seems like endless shallow grade miles, gradually gaining in altitude. Towards the top there is a just over five miles in length section of more solid grade. The route has a true alpine feel here as the road begins to twist up the hill on this final stretch of climbing. Soon some of the sharp peaks of the Uintah Range are in view as you close in on the summit. Towards the very top the grade eases and the ascent ends at the signed top in spectacular surroundings at well over 10,000 feet of elevation (top portion closed in winter - Uinta-Wasatch-Cache National Forest - (801) 466-6411).

Climb Stats:

Total elevation - 4,253 ft	**Length - 29.0 miles**
Average Grade - 2.8% (8%)	**Time - 90-150 minutes**

Directions - On Route 32 in Kamas, head east on Route 150 to the east edge of town to begin the climb by continuing east.

BALD MTN.
PASS

Wolf Creek Summit East

Category 2

The east side of Wolf Creek Summit along Route 35 is a somewhat isolated climb located northwest of Duchesne that begins from a high altitude valley. The route follows a drainage for much of its length and is scenic and over a mostly moderate grade as well. Exposed for almost its entire distance, there are good views of the surrounding mountains in places as you near the signed summit and the climb ends at high altitude in a tree lined meadow.

The hill begins by heading west away from the North Fork of the Duchesne River over pretty shallow grade and with little traffic. As you gain altitude the tree cover begins to take on a more alpine look. The grade gradually increases with the elevation as well but is quite steady for long sections throughout. There is an over two mile long stretch within its upper half that is more stout and is the most difficult pedaling on the hill. The grade over the final mile eases a bit as the road begins to follow more graceful curves up the mountainside. You travel through true alpine meadows along this stretch as well. Towards the very top of the climb the grade eases further and the ascent ends within a pleasant setting at the signed (elevation only) summit at over 9,000 feet (closed in winter - Uinta-Wasatch-Cache National Forest - (435) 654-0470).

Climb Stats:

Total elevation - 2,328 ft | **Length - 10.1 miles**

Average Grade - 4.4% (8%) | **Time - 45-90 minutes**

Directions - From Tabiona, UT on Route 35, head west on 35 for ~9 miles to the North Fork of the Duchesne River to begin the climb by continuing west on Route 35.

Wolf Creek Summit West

Category 2

The west side of Wolf Creek Summit is a bit shorter than its eastern side but carries a more solid overall grade. The pedaling is over variable and mostly moderate slope for much of the ride although like the eastern side it has a section of steeper climbing to negotiate. There are good views of the surrounding mountains in places along the way as well.

From the Nobletts Trailhead parking area the road heads generally east along moderate grade and a scenic route with little traffic most days. One mile into your climb you will encounter a fairly long section of flat/descending riding. Uphill soon resumes for good as you cross the bridge over the South Fork of the Provo River over more solid grade which is a bit variable. The road seems to narrow at this point as it swings through gentle curves with tighter tree cover as well. Several miles from the river crossing the slope picks up precipitously and larger trees are now part of the landscape. The more challenging grade continues for almost 3 miles as you steadily gain altitude along a ridgeline in places. Towards the very top stout pedaling finally eases as true high mountain scenery comes into view. The ascent ends soon after at the signed summit at over 9,000 feet of elevation (closed in winter - Uinta-Wasatch-Cache National Forest - 435 654-0470).

Climb Stats:

Total elevation - 2,009 ft | **Length - 7.3 miles**

Average Grade - 5.2% (11%) | **Time - 30-60 minutes**

Directions - On Route 35 in tiny Francis, UT head east on 35 for just over 12 miles to the Nobletts Trailhead (parking on left) to begin the listed climb by continuing east up the hill.

8%

44 North

Category 2

The climb of 44 North is a bit difficult to get to but well worth the effort. It carries a solid grade all the way up its scenic slopes and you have very nice views of the Flaming Gorge Reservoir as you ascend. In addition, you should encounter little traffic and few if any cyclists along the way. You might say this hill has it all so enjoy the ride.

The ascent begins as you ride east over moderate grade with views of the reservoir to your left. Soon you pass the road to Sheeps Creek Bay and the slope picks up such that you are working hard over the steepest sustained climbing on the hill. After approximately one mile of stout grade you get a slight break as the gradient eases but keep in mind there is really not any shallow slope on this hill. This section curves along a ridgeline with very nice scenery. There is some exposure in places to keep you on your toes as well. As you approach the top the grade picks up again for a stretch but the blue reservoir and pink and yellow rocks all around you can help ease any pain you may be experiencing. Towards the very end of your ride you find the grade easing and the climb ends at an unmarked summit just beyond a cut through a large ridge of yellow rock. From here the road continues uphill intermittently and over shallow grade after a descent but significant climbing has ended.

Climb Stats:

Total elevation - 1,627 ft | **Length - 4.7 miles**

Average Grade - 6.6% (9%) | **Time - 20-40 minutes**

Directions - In Manilla, UT head south on Route 44 for ~9 miles to begin the listed climb as the road exits a canyon as a descent ends and the route begins to ascend.

191 North

Category 2

The north side of Route 191 carries riders through the isolated northeast corner of the state. It does not top out at the signed pass as there are multiple descents towards that point. The road travels through part of the scenic Flaming Gorge National Recreation Area as well as national forest land to reach high altitude. There are no surprises on this one as the grade is shallow to moderate throughout. You will not likely see any other riders on this hill and little traffic.

Pull away from the interesting bridge over the Green River on fairly solid grade to begin this climb. The road is somewhat twisty and there are views of the scenic reservoir in places. Soon you pass the Flaming Gorge Resort on the right where the grade decreases significantly. It quickly picks back up as the route then begins to stair step up the hill through a pine forest. Just over 5 miles into your assault, turn left at the junction with Route 44 to continue up the hill to the south. The grade from this point is variable and mostly moderate for the remainder of the ride. There are no surprises on this section and this listed hill ends where you leave the Flaming Gorge Recreation Area (pull out on left and large sign facing south). From this point the road goes up and down for ~7 miles to a signed pass but significant climbing has ended.

Climb Stats:

Total elevation - 1,988 ft | **Length - 7.7 miles**

Average Grade - 4.9% (7%) | **Time - 35-70 minutes**

Directions - On Route 191 within the Flaming Gorge Recreation Area head to the bridge over the Green River to begin the climb by heading west on Route 191.

FLAMING GORGE
National
Recreation Area
U.S. FOREST SERVICE
BUREAU OF RECLAMATION

191 South

Category 1

The south side of Route 191 is a somewhat difficult climb to altitude along a solid grade. It brings riders toward Flaming Gorge Recreation Area in a quite isolated setting. The overall grade can make you work for the top and the interesting scenery will help you get there.

The climb begins with two lanes going uphill and over shallow slope. Quickly you encounter a turn to the left. The grade then increases as this is the beginning of a large switchback. The right hander soon follows and then another turn to the left. You find stout pedaling here and as the road straightens a bit further up the hill, the slope increases a bit more. You pass a mine on the left on this stretch and then the switchbacks resume and a few trees appear as you gain altitude. Many may work hard to get through this section. Steadily gaining in altitude, you then enter the national forest where the slope finally eases. Soon you follow a ridgeline for a time as the grade gradually builds back up to more challenging. Crossing a cattleguard the stout slope returns for a final time. The slope finally decreases and the listed climb ends soon after at the junction with Red Cloud Loop on the left. You can continue north on 191 for another 6 miles through mountain meadows up to the actual pass over mostly shallow up and down riding.

Climb Stats:

Total elevation - 2,576 ft **Length - 8.9 miles**
Average Grade - 5.5% (8%) **Time - 40-90 minutes**

Directions - In Vernal, UT at the junction of Routes 40 and 191, head north on Route 191 for 12.5 miles to begin the climb (unmarked start) by continuing north as the grade picks up.

8%

Salt Lake/Provo/Midway

City Creek Canyon

Category 2

City Creek is the in town climb in Salt Lake City. Be careful of the average grade as it does provide greater challenge over its upper half along with a pastoral setting (and restrooms every mile or so). Along one of the most narrow roads you can imagine, you may encounter a few hikers on the route and light if any traffic; in fact you likely need only to keep an eye out for the regular vehicle patrols by park staff. Keep in mind City Creek Canyon is only currently open to bikes on odd days of the week (this policy has changed over the years so you may want to check first before riding this one).

From the tollbooth, head north up the drainage over quite shallow grade with views of the surrounding hills. The slope goes up and down on this hill constantly such that you are riding over solid stretches and then small descents. Just over one mile in, you find more solid climbing. It is short lived however and soon you are back to up and down riding on the narrow road. Eventually thick trees close in which can be helpful on warm days. Just over 3 miles into your foray you pass a water plant on the right and the road narrows even further if that is possible. The grade, while still variable, picks up here. Towards the end of your ride you encounter the steepest sustained climbing on the hill. The ascent soon ends quite suddenly as the pavement ends in pleasant surroundings.

Climb Stats:

Total elevation - 1,433 ft **Length - 5.5 miles**
Average Grade - 4.9% (11%) **Time - 20-40 minutes**

Directions - In Salt Lake City the climb begins at the junction of City Creek Canyon Road and Bonneville Boulevard (toll gate).

Emigration Canyon

Category 3

Another in town climb (at least to start), Emigration Canyon is a Salt Lake City landmark and carries riders out of the city basin and toward mountain peaks. You will ride through a tunnel of trees and a small community along the way before the trees recede near the top within a somewhat alpine setting. Quite shallow down low, your work comes as you run into more stout climbing close to the summit.

Begin the ascent by heading east on Emigration Canyon Road over shallow grade and a bit of congestion. You glide by a few high rise apartments on your right as you ride into the canyon. City clutter gradually fades away as you gain altitude (albeit slowly). A few houses then appear as the grade remains shallow some distance into the ascent. You then ride through a small elongated village without significant elevation change. Around 6 miles into the assault, make a tight right hand turn as the trees recede and the grade increases (you can also turn left here for several miles of stout climbing to a deadend). From this point you encounter solid slope and longer views. A left hand turn lines you up for the finishing straight which takes riders up to the obvious summit with more expansive vistas. You can continue east and descend to the south side of Big Mountain (subsequent climb) and there is parking at the top.

Climb Stats:

Total elevation - 1,311 ft | **Length - 7.8 miles**

Average Grade - 3.2% (8%) | **Time - 25-60 minutes**

Directions - In Salt Lake City the climb begins at the junction of Emigration Canyon Road and Crestview Drive in the southeast portion of the city by heading east on Emigration Canyon Road.

East Canyon

Category 2

The climb of East Canyon is a very scenic and challenging in places ascent along Route 65 located just east of Salt Lake City. Its start is somewhat isolated but it is worth the effort to get there. You will ride over a variable grade and a somewhat narrow road for much of its length and the hill contains mountain views in places along with a quite solid finish. Traffic is typically light and you should see a few riders on this hill on good weather weekends.

A shallow start, you head into woods quite quickly as you ride generally south towards the summit. The grade gradually picks up to more challenging but is never particularly steep on this hill. Several miles into the ascent you encounter a switchback that requires some effort to get through along with thicker tree cover beyond. A bit later the slope eases and the roadway becomes quite twisty and nice views appear in places. Soon a descent/flat occurs which lasts for about a half mile before climbing resumes over fairly solid grade. The narrow road takes on an alpine feel along this section as you ride through mostly thick woods which part in places with a few views. The grade continues as solid right up to the obvious summit at the Salt Lake County line in a pleasant setting. East Canyon is a fun descent as well.

Climb Stats:

Total elevation - 1,603 ft	**Length - 5.4 miles**
Average Grade - 5.6% (8%)	**Time - 25-45 minutes**

Directions - From Interstate 84 in Henefer, UT, take Route 65 south for a distance to East Canyon Reservoir. Just south of the reservoir the listed climb begins by continuing south on 65 as the grade increases.

Big Mountain

Category 2

The opposite side of East Canyon (previous climb), Big Mountain heads up Route 65 along initially mild and then challenging grade. Quite popular with local peak baggers, it can lead to other riding/climbing nearby. Don't let the average grade fool you on this one as the hill provides a solid finishing stretch along with pleasant mountain views.

A shallow start, you have nice views of the Wasatch as you pull away from Interstate 80, soon to find more solid slope. In a short time you pass the east side of the climb of Emigration Canyon on your left (dam and parking area on the right) as the grade eases. Beyond this junction the grade picks up a bit (but is not steep) and more trees appear along the route, giving it a more alpine feel. The road narrows and takes a mostly straight (to the north) routing on this section which can produce speed on the descent. Soon the more stout side of Big Mountain shows itself as just under 4 miles into the climb pedaling changes significantly. This final stretch is along solid grade (last 3.8 miles average just under 7%) and through several tree-lined switchbacks as you ride up the shoulder of the mountain. At least the grade is quite steady on this section as you must now concentrate to reach the summit. Near the top some nice views appear and the climb ends at the Morgan County line.

Climb Stats:

Total elevation - 1,881 ft	**Length - 7.5 miles**
Average Grade - 4.8% (10%)	**Time - 30-60 minutes**

Directions - From Interstate 80 just east of Salt Lake City, head north on Route 65 for a short distance to begin the climb where the descent down from the interstate ends.

SHARE
THE
ROAD

Millcreek Canyon

Category 1

Another hill close to Salt Lake City, Millcreek Canyon is a big climb over moderate and variable grade within one of the most popular outdoor venues in the area. It contains several flats along the way for recovery which lessen the overall average grade. You can find some solitude on the tree lined slopes although it can still be quite busy on weekends. The pavement ends at its summit in a very scenic setting.

Shallow to begin, you ride along a shady street to the east. After a half mile you will pass the tollbooth (no cost for bikes) to enter the park. Soon you encounter the first more solid ramp of climbing as rock walls loom over you. The stout grade does not last long however as you quickly return to more moderate riding. You pass multiple trailheads along the way with some congestion at times, particularly on the weekends. Soon the tree cover thickens and the road narrows, giving an alpine feel. The grade has gradually steepened as you have gained altitude but it will continue to be variable right up to climb end. Near the summit you find a short section of double digit slope and the climb soon ends at a parking area in a very beautiful setting (closed in winter - Uinta-Wasatch-Cache National Forest 801 733-2660).

Climb Stats:

Total elevation - 2,412 ft **Length - 9.0 miles**

Average Grade - 5.1% (14%) **Time - 45-90 minutes**

Directions - From Wasatch Boulevard in Salt Lake City head east on E 3800 S for 0.2 miles (becomes Millcreek Canyon Road) to its junction with Parkview Drive to begin the climb by continuing east into Millcreek Canyon.

Big Cottonwood Canyon

Category 1

The climb up Big Cottonwood Canyon (Route 190) is one of the most difficult in Utah. Reaching high altitude Guardsman Pass, it is over a route that does carry some ski traffic and others on good weather weekends. Quite popular, you will likely have some company up at least part of this big hill.

A shallow start turns a bit steeper when the road gets very twisty. Soon the route straightens as you head higher between big rock walls. Keep heading east and just beyond the five mile mark the grade eases a bit through its middle section. Just over 12 miles in are two more solid grade miles and then you turn sharply left for the pass (keep straight to reach the Brighton Ski Resort). The first ramp on this final section is steeper (double digit briefly) and the slope then eases a bit. The upper part of the ascent is scenic and over variable grade (one more short double digit grade section) and the climb soon ends at dramatic Guardsman Pass with its access to mountain biking and hiking (upper section closed in winter - Uinta-Wasatch-Cache National Forest - 801 733-2660). The descent is challenging in places so be alert, particularly the tight curves just before and as you join the main road and down low where there are many areas where people park just off of the road to hike/climb.

Climb Stats:

Total elevation - 4,814 ft | **Length - 17.1 miles**

Average Grade - 5.3% (12%) | **Time - 70-120 minutes**

Directions - From Interstate 80 in Salt Lake City take Exit 7 and go south on Wasatch Boulevard for a short distance to Route 190. The climb begins at the junction by heading east on 190.

Little Cottonwood Canyon

Category 1

Little Cottonwood Canyon is a challenging and scenic climb located just southeast of Salt Lake City. One of the most difficult in the state, the hill carries riders toward multiple ski areas into the Wasatch Mountains and within a steep walled canyon and is a favorite of those looking to test themselves on a big hill. Called by some the most dangerous road in the United States (avalanches), the steepest climbing on this one is over its bottom half.

Immediately you are thrust between big mountain walls to begin the ascent along with intermittent traffic most days. The slope is solid but not steep to start but soon gets steeper and approaches 10% for an extended stretch, the most difficult pedaling on the hill. As you climb higher the road leads uphill through gentle turns along the north side of the drainage. Ski areas eventually appear, first Snowbird and then Alta as the grade eases as you pedal higher. The superb alpine scenery will help you to the top and the hill ends at the top of a parking area within a scenic bowl just above the Alta Resort (pavement turns to dirt). The descent of Little Cottonwood is one of the quickest you will find as its mostly gentle curves seem to funnel you down the hill with big speed.

Climb Stats:

Total elevation - 3,390 ft	**Length - 8.6 miles**
Average Grade - 7.5% (10%)	**Time - 35-75 minutes**

Directions - From Interstate 15 in Sandy, UT go east on E 9000 S which eventually becomes S Little Cottonwood Road to reach Route 210. The climb begins there by heading east on 210 into the canyon.

Traverse Ridge Road

Category 2

Traverse Ridge Road is a stout climb located just south of the town of Draper. It is over a solid overall grade as it is one of the steepest ascents in Utah. The hill does carry some traffic on its slopes and has some congestion in a few places but the roadway is wide so there is plenty of room to ride most of the time. The annual Tour of Utah has used this hill as a descent multiple times over the years.

From the stoplight you begin the ascent over shallow grade and you will very likely head up the hill with some traffic to accompany you. In fact, there are a number of residences and businesses on this lower section so it may be a good idea to keep an eye out for turning vehicles as you climb higher. Just under one mile in, the grade pops up to quite stout as the road expands to 4 lanes. Climb for one mile and then you will encounter a short descent and flat where you can catch your breath. Climbing soon resumes over again stout grade as you continue to move further up the mountain. Just before the summit the grade eases as the road intersects with Suncrest Drive to end the listed climb. Due to its grade and routing Traverse Ridge Road is a quite quick in places descent as well so enjoy the ride (and the long views up top) on the way down.

Climb Stats:

Total elevation - 1,302 ft **Length - 3.5 miles**

Average Grade - 7.1% (10%) **Time - 20-30 minutes**

Directions - In the growing community of Draper, UT from the busy intersection of Highland Drive and Traverse Ridge Road, head south on four lane Traverse Ridge Road to begin the listed climb.

10%
NO
HUNTING
WITHIN
CITY
LIMITS

Suncrest Drive

Category 2

The opposite side of the previous ascent (Traverse Ridge Road), Suncrest Drive, while a bit longer and less steep, is a somewhat similar climb. The road carries riders away from Orem and American Fork in a stair step fashion along with a bit of traffic at times. Over 4 lanes, there is room to ride however and its treeless expanses provide long views to the east and south. It is over a fairly solid grade and has been used in the annual Tour of Utah by the professionals.

The initial pedaling on Suncrest is over quite shallow grade as you head north up the hill. Just over one half mile into the ascent you hit more stout slope and the longest stretch of challenging grade on the mountain. Keep turning the pedals and after another 1.4 miles the grade eases, soon gets stout again and then eases again as the road becomes divided. Quickly you encounter another solid section followed shortly by more shallow climbing. Ascending then resumes as gradually stout for a final stretch amid increased development and congestion and the climb ends at the intersection with Haddington Road just before you reach a major intersection. Suncrest Drive is a quite quick descent if speed is what you are seeking.

Climb Stats:

Total elevation - 1,167 ft | **Length - 3.9 miles**

Average Grade - 5.7% (10%) | **Time - 20-30 minutes**

Directions - From the junction of busy Route 92 and Highland Boulevard in rapidly expanding Highland, UT, head north on Highland for 1.2 miles to begin the listed climb at its junction with 800 N on the right by continuing north up the hill on what is now Suncrest Drive.

8%

Alpine Summit East

Category 1

The east side of Alpine Summit (Route 92) located northeast of Provo is a true gem. At times used by the professionals in the annual Tour of Utah, the climb is over stout overall grade as it cuts through the mighty Wasatch and passes by the Sundance Resort. It is also one of the most scenic in the state but keep in mind it is a solid category 1 ascent so you would do well not to underestimate this one. From its narrow routing along tree lined slopes to its big mountain views this hill has it all.

The start is within a canyon along fairly stout grade (steepest sustained climbing on the route) and you will soon ride past the resort on the left as the slope eases. Over two lanes below the resort, just beyond, the road reduces to a wide single lane and the true nature of this amazing ascent is revealed. With majestic Mount Timpanogos visible briefly in front of you, the road then disappears into the trees as it begins to twist up the ridge through graceful curves. You will ride over fairly steady grade for much of the remainder of the ascent. It gets very tight and twisty in places and passes through one of the largest grove of aspens the author as ever seen. The climb ends at an unmarked but obvious summit at a hiking trailhead (closed in winter - Uinta-Wasatch-Cache National Forest - 801 785-3563).

Climb Stats:

Total elevation - 2,836 ft | **Length - 8.7 miles**

Average Grade - 6.2% (10%) | **Time - 40-75 minutes**

Directions - From Orem, UT head north on Route 189 towards Heber into Provo Canyon. After ~7 miles Route 92 will appear (suddenly) on the left and the climb begins at the junction.

Alpine Summit West

Category 1

The west side of Alpine Summit (Route 92) is a bit longer and more shallow than its east side and is a true category 1 climb. It is also among the most scenic in Utah. The initial section is within a canyon and tree lined and passes through Timpanogos Cave National Monument along the way. As such, there may be a few vehicles on this lower stretch as thicker traffic for the entire route is typically restricted to good weather weekends. The grade gradually increases as you ride generally east, following a creek up canyon on this section.

Soon the road turns right and seemingly more directly up the mountain, tending to get more twisty as you gain altitude. A large switchback to the left then leads into an open section that is exceptionally scenic with some eventual exposure to your right. Mountain views soon recede as the upper part of the ascent enters the trees including large stands of aspens and continues over solid grade. The route then begins to switchback a bit through thick woods as climbing continues. Near the very top the grade eases and the ascent ends at an unmarked but obvious pass within a huge grove of aspen trees (closed in winter - Uinta-Wastch-Cache National Forest - 801 785-3563).

Climb Stats:

Total elevation - 2,980 ft	**Length - 10.7 miles**
Average Grade - 5.3% (9%)	**Time - 40-75 minutes**

Directions - From Interstate 15 just north of American Fork head east on Route 92 (Timpanogos Highway) for ~7 miles to Canyon Road on the right. Continue east on Route 92 and the climb begins just beyond after you enter the canyon.

Squaw Peak

Category 2

Squaw Peak is a relatively short and stout climb very close to the Orem/Provo area over a somewhat narrow and twisty roadway. It carries solid grade over most of its route and traffic is usually quite light on this hill. It has some real bite to its end but also provides spectacular and long views down into the large valley to the west.

The hill begins as moderate but then rears up to stout grade for a short stretch. A short section is particularly troublesome but then the grade eases as you eventually enter a valley with pleasant scenery. From this point the road twists up the valley over mostly solid grade with views of Squaw Peak right in front of you for parts of the ascent. As you gain altitude there are long views to your right in places and increased tree cover although the hill is exposed over almost its entire length. Closer to the summit the grade pops back up to double digit for a sustained stretch as you bear to the right to reach the overlook and summit. The final half mile seems to go on forever but just keep the pedals turning and you should make the top. The ascent ends at an unmarked but obvious top (small parking area) at over 6,600 feet of elevation with very long views (closed in winter - Uinta-Wasatch-Cache National Forest - 801 785-3563).

Climb Stats:

Total elevation - 1,548 ft	**Length - 4.3 miles**
Average Grade - 6.8 (13%)	**Time - 25-45 minutes**

Directions - In Orem, UT at the junction of Route 189 and E800N head northeast on Route 189 into Provo Canyon for ~2 miles to Squaw Peak Road on the right where the climb begins.

Guardsman Pass East

Beyond Category

A recent gift to cyclists (the upper stretches of this one were paved in 2011 and 2012), the east side of mighty Guardsman Pass south of Park City is very likely the most difficult climb in the state of Utah and is one of the most difficult in the United States. It rises up from the town of Midway over a steep south facing mountain slope and through scenic stands of aspens along the way. It is along a quite variable grade as you will need to negotiate double digit grade ramps as well as a few flats/descents. A majority of its route was introduced to cyclists through the 2012 Tour of Utah (and top pro Levi Leiphiemer) and although those riders did not go up and over Guardsman Pass, (they used nearby and lower elevation Empire Pass to get back Park City to finish the stage) viewers could certainly tell the hill is a stiff test.

A modest beginning in a spectacular setting soon leads to steeper grade as you leave signs of civilization behind and begin to twist up the hill from the road junction. The first double digit grade ramp arrives just under a mile into the ascent. Thick trees (many aspens) soon greet you as you climb higher. The grade on this hill is quite variable as the multiple sections of double digit pedaling are mostly fairly short and followed by lesser slope although the constant variability adds to the hill's difficulty. A twisty route with multiple switchbacks somewhat prevents you from seeing the agony to come although you can generally sense the wall of rock and difficult climbing ahead of you. Around 3.5 miles in you reach another ramp of steep grade that contains the maximum grade on the ascent. The slope then eases and soon you come to the first of two short descents, which occur fairly close together.

Once beyond the first, the grade picks back up quickly and touches double digit, eases and then gets back up to double digit again briefly before the final descent. It is short and from that

10%
12
NEXT
1½ MILES
12

point you have less than a mile of still solid grade up to a junction. The trees part just before the junction and this affords excellent views of the high altitude mountain slopes around you. From here head to the left to immediately encounter another double digit ramp that lasts for just over one half mile and that is over slightly rougher pavement. The grade then eases a bit before steepening again for a short stretch. Just before the summit the grade eases for a final time as you encounter exposure to your left. Just beyond you reach high altitude and impressive Guardsman Pass with its access to hiking and with biking and excellent views to the east. This is also the top of the Big Cottonwood Canyon climb from the west side of the pass (see the Salt Lake City/Provo/ Midway section of this guide). Make sure to pat yourself on the back when you reach the summit of this giant hill as you will have earned it.

As mentioned, Guardsman Pass East is among the most difficult of American climbs and likely the most difficult in the state of Utah so make sure you are prepared before you tackle this one. Although the summit does not have a lot of room it would be ideal if its top may one day be visited by top professionals in the Tour of Utah as a stage finish. Regardless, it is a true prize in American cycling climbing. Due to its steep grade and many tight switchbacks its descent may be challenging in places as well (upper section closed in winter - Wasatch-Cache National Forest - 801 733-2660).

Climb Stats:

Total elevation - 3,948 ft	**Length - 8.6 miles**
Average Grade - 8.7% (18%)	**Time - 45-90 minutes**

Directions - In Midway, UT south of Park City get to Pine Canyon Road on the north side of town. Continue northwest on Pine Canyon Road until it ends at Warm Springs Drive. The climb begins here by continuing north up the hill

Empire Pass North

Category 1

The north side of Empire Pass is a steep and scenic climb away from and then above spectacular Park City. Popular among area riders, keep in mind it is a difficult ascent and its descent has been used by the professionals in the annual Tour of Utah. The grade begins as shallow with some traffic in usually busy Park City and gradually gets steeper. At mile 1.4 bear right onto Marzaac to find fewer vehicles, less congestion, steepening grade and more alpine scenery; what might be considered a perfect combination for riding.

Continue riding along now stout grade and then you encounter a short descent just over 3 miles into the climb. Uphill riding then resumes over moderate grade among stands of trees and groups of condominiums scattered among the mountain slopes. The slope gradually gets steeper until a traffic circle at a resort where the slope flattens out. From there steep grade returns for the final mile of climbing which includes a few large switchbacks through scenic aspens and mountain homes. Near the very top the grade eases as you seem to leave all signs of civilization behind. The summit is obvious and offers large views towards the south and of the surrounding mountains.

Climb Stats:

Total elevation - 2,094 ft **Length - 5.6 miles**

Average Grade - 7.1% (12%) **Time - 30-60 minutes**

Directions - In Park City, UT the listed climb begins at the junction of Bonanza and Deer Valley Drive by heading up Deer Valley Drive (there are several other starts in town that will produce similar statistics).

10%
NEXT
1 1/2 MILE
BRAKE CHECK
ALL TRUCKS
OVER 10,000 G.V.W.
MUST STOP
MILE
3

Empire Pass South

Category 1

One of the most difficult climbs in Utah, the south side of Empire Pass is a stout test that has seen professional cyclists race on its slopes (the 2012 and 2013 Tours of Utah used this ascent in the final race stage to finish in Park City). The hill shares most of its length with the east side of mighty Guardsman Pass (prior page). Begin over that ascent's variable grade and difficult slopes with its many tight turns and steep ramps. Hopefully the large aspen stands you ride through will remain for many years to come as well. Towards the top of this very difficult stretch you reach a junction at mile 6.9.

From the high altitude junction, turn right to continue (turn left for the east side of Guardsman Pass; prior climb). After the turn you immediately find moderate grade and soon a flat followed by a short descent. The trees have parted here to reveal long and spectacular mountain views on clear days. Climbing then quickly resumes for a short distance over moderate grade up to the unmarked but obvious summit at high elevation. There is limited parking at the top and of course you can descend from here into the mountain berg of Park City to the north (upper section closed in winter - Wasatch-Cache National Forest - 801 733-2660).

Climb Stats:

Total elevation - 3,181 ft	**Length - 7.7 miles**
Average Grade - 7.8% (18%)	**Time - 40-90 minutes**

Directions - In Midway, UT south of Park City get to Pine Canyon Road on the north side of town. Continue northwest on Pine Canyon Road until it ends at Warm Springs Drive. The climb begins here by continuing north up the hill.

ATTENTION
NO SEMIS
ALLOWED
(MOUNTAIN ROAD)
1369

Snake Creek Road

Category 2

Snake Creek Road is a fairly short and solid grade climb from the pleasant and scenic town of Midway. It begins at a golf course at the edge of town and ends as the road turns to dirt in an isolated setting. The grade is variable for much of the ride and it includes a section of double digit slope along the way. As of 2013 the pavement goes from smooth and brand new in places to quite old and cracked in others. Tree lined for much of the route, there are good views of the surrounding mountains in places over its length.

The climb begins over fairly shallow grade with the golf course to your right. The road, which initially took you generally north, soon swings to the left towards the west and trees eventually close in. Just over a mile into the ascent a few buildings appear, including one quite close to the road to the left, along with increased grade. With one mile to go you will run into a ramp of double digit slope which lasts for about a half mile. At that point the grade eases a bit but also becomes quite variable. Just before the summit the slope eases further and the climb ends as the pavement ends at a junction with two gravel roads which can take people further up the mountain. The descent of Snake Creek Road is a fast one in places and there is good mountain biking in the area as well.

Climb Stats:

Total elevation - 1,035 ft	**Length - 3.3 miles**
Average Grade - 5.9% (14%)	**Time - 20-40 minutes**

Directions - In Midway, UT get to the junction of 1100N (Cari Lane) and 700 W (Homestead Road). Head north on 700 W (now Snake Creek Road) for a very short distance to begin.

FALLING
ROCK

Central Utah

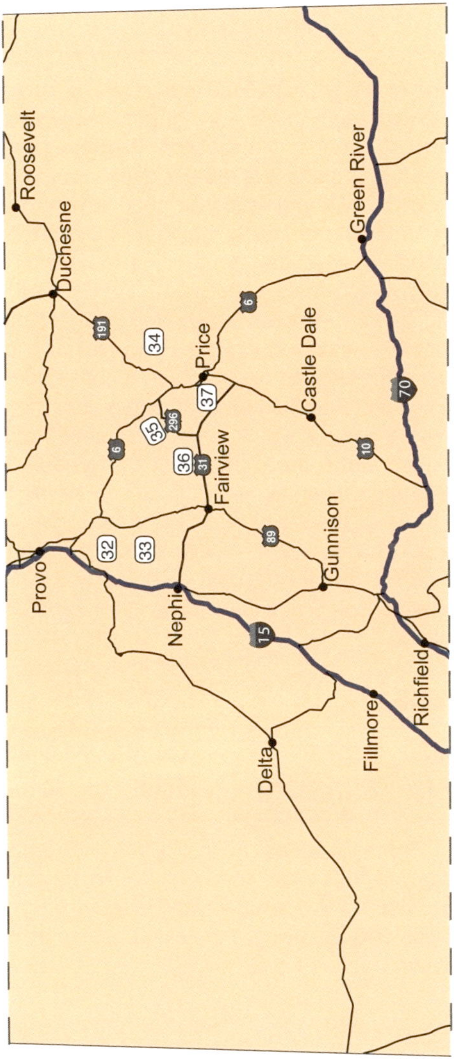

Nebo Loop Road North

Category 1

The north side of Nebo Loop Road is a very long and somewhat shallow climb just south of Payson. It has been graced by the professionals in the Tour of Utah as well. Beginning as you leave the suburbs of town behind, the route is over a narrow and twisty road which can carry some traffic on good weather weekends. The grade is variable and mostly moderate for much of the ride. There are good views of the surrounding mountains in places over its length.

The climb begins in scrub brush and over mostly shallow grade as you ride south. Soon the slope picks up along with the tree cover and the road begins to switchback somewhat up the mountain. The route then tends to curve along the ridgeline over less steep slope. Towards the top is a series of descents/ flats which knock down the climb's average grade. There are also very good high mountain views in places as the trees thin. The ascent ends at the signed summit at well over 9,000 feet of elevation (closed in winter - Uinta-Wasatch-Cache National Forest - 435 623-2735). It's descent is challenging in places and there is good mountain biking in the area as well.

Climb Stats:

Total elevation - 4,506 ft	**Length - 22.0 miles**
Average Grade - 3.9% (10%)	**Time - 75-150 minutes**

Directions - From Interstate 15 in Payson, UT take exit 252 and head east on 800 south for 1.3 miles to Payson Canyon Road (right). Head up Payson Canyon Road for 0.7 miles to its intersection with 600 East where the climb begins by continuing south on Payson Canyon Road.

Nebo Loop Road South

Category 1

Used several times by the professionals in the always difficult Tour of Utah road race, the south side of Nebo Loop Road is a category 1 rated climb up the massive slopes of Mount Nebo in central Utah. This mountain really looms over the entire area so an opportunity to take a road bike high on its slopes is one that certainly should be taken advantage of. The hill provides it all in that it is a long climb with big mountain views and challenging grade in places.

Straight and somewhat shallow to start, the grade soon picks up as the road begins to switchback up the hill. Excellent views are present back down to climb start if you can appreciate them. Just over 5 miles into the ascent is a big turn to the right with increased (double digit) grade for an extended stretch, the most challenging climbing on the hill. Eventually the slope eases as the road continues to twist over the mountain generally towards the north with long vistas. As you approach the top you will encounter increased tree cover in places and a more variable grade that includes several descents which knock down the hill's average grade. The climb soon ends at the signed summit at over 9,000 feet of elevation (closed in winter - Uinta-Wasatch-Cache National Forest - 435 623-2735).

Climb Stats:

Total elevation - 3,564 ft | **Length - 13.8 miles**

Average Grade - 4.9% (12%) | **Time - 60-100 minutes**

Directions - From Interstate 15 in Nephi, UT head east on Route 132 for several miles to Nebo Loop Road on the left where the listed climb begins.

Indian Canyon South

Category 2

The south side of Indian Canyon on Route 191 is a fairly long ascent located northeast of Price. The route passes a coal facility at climb start and is over a somewhat narrow and twisty in places road that carries little traffic most days. The grade is variable and mostly moderate for much of the ride. However, while it is fairly shallow overall, don't let the average grade fool you on this one. It is a tale of two climbs in a sense and ends at altitude in an isolated setting.

The hill begins by leaving the coal production and soon an old graveyard on the left behind along a drainage and over shallow grade. This section then begins to twist a bit, gradually getting steeper before a turn to the left occurs as you leave the canyon and enter a small valley. The grade remains moderate here although gradually steepening in general. After just over 10 miles of climbing the hill takes a different turn as you encounter alternate conditions. The grade kicks up here to quite stout and your pleasant ride is over for the day as the final 4.5 miles average 7% grade through a classic stretch of road bike climbing. Trees appear in places as you gain attitude via a winding and somewhat narrow road. The slope eases near the top and the ascent ends at the signed summit at over 9,000 feet of elevation with long views in places.

Climb Stats:

Total elevation - 3,012 ft	**Length - 14.9 miles**
Average Grade - 3.8% (8%)	**Time - 60-100 minutes**

Directions - At the junction of Routes 6 and 191 west of Price, head north on Route 191 for 0.2 miles (just beyond the coal plant) to begin the climb by continuing north.

SUMMIT
9114 FT.

264 East

Category 2

The east side of Route 264 is an isolated climb located west of the town of Price that reaches high altitude at its summit. Carrying a solid overall grade, it follows a coal conveyor belt up the hill over part of its route which is quite unique. The pedaling is over mostly steady slope for the majority of the hill and the route is a pleasant one through scenic surroundings. In addition, the road sees little traffic and few cyclists most of the time it appears.

This climb begins over pretty solid grade as you head west up the hill as the route follows a drainage within a small canyon with a swift creek to your left. Shortly a coal conveyor crosses over the road and the chute then parallels your route above the road on the right for some distance. The grade has increased since climb start such that now you are riding over stout slope but it is fairly steady so you should be able to get into a rhythm on this section. Eventually you reach the coal mine that is the source of the conveyor system. Above the mine the grade eases a bit and the route takes on a more alpine look and feel. You eventually ride through a big S bend as you steadily gain altitude into a scenic aspen forest closer to the summit. Towards the very end the slope eases further and the climb ends in isolation at the Carbon/Emory County lines in a very pleasant setting. The descent of 264 East is an interesting one as well

Climb Stats:

Total elevation - 1,492 ft | **Length - 4.8 miles**

Average Grade - 5.9% (9%) | **Time - 25-40 minutes**

Directions - From the isolated junction of Routes 264 and 96 several miles south of Scofield, UT, head west on 264 to begin the listed climb.

31 East

Category 2

The east side of Route 31 is a long and interesting climb up into the high country of central Utah on a road that sees little traffic (and cyclists) most of the time. It follows a drainage up into the mountains and is over mostly shallow grade. The route's chief attribute may be the scenery you will encounter as you ride higher. The top reaches quite high elevation and is also an isolated summit.

You quickly leave the monstrous plant behind at climb start as you head west to follow a small water way over shallow to moderate grade. Soon you enter a canyon with increased scenery and then the national forest as the creek in the drainage becomes more visible to your left. The canyon gets quite twisty in places and the grade increases just a bit. Eventually heavier tree cover arrives giving a more alpine feel to the climb. Higher up, aspens arrive and you will pass a small lake on the right. Soon you pass through a large aspen forest and a larger lake on the left. Along the way the grade continues to be quite mild for most of your effort. Towards the very top the slope eases and the trees thin, creating open meadows. The climb ends soon after at just under 10,000 feet at the signed summit within an alpine and isolated setting.

Climb Stats:

Total elevation - 3,685 ft	**Length - 26.3 miles**
Average Grade - 2.7% (7%)	**Time - 90-150 minutes**

Directions - From the junction of Routes 31 and 10 in the small town of Huntington, UT take Route 31 west for several miles to the power plant on the left to begin the listed climb by continuing west on Route 31.

31 West

Category 1

The west side of Route 31 is a difficult climb up into the high country of central Utah on a road that sees little traffic most of the time. In fact it is one of the most difficult climbs in the state but most of the uphill is over quite steady grade. The road carries the rider from high valley views into a canyon and then to high altitude panoramas as it reaches up to almost 10,000 feet of elevation at the end of the route.

The climb begins in the small town of Fairview over fairly solid grade. Quickly leaving town you enter a drainage which cuts off views and the grade increases along this section as well. This is the key stretch of climbing along the route as you wind up the canyon through multiple turns. Further on you enter the national forest where the grade eases. Soon it pops back up to where it was previously. Around 8 miles into the ascent you exit the canyon and the grade eases. Quickly you pass Route 264 on the left but keep straight. Here the scenery becomes more alpine with the increased altitude. Aspens appear as the grade now begins to stair step up the hill. Towards the top the slope eases and the climb ends at just under 10,000 feet at the intersection with Skyline Drive (signed dirt road on the right) in a high mountain and isolated setting. It's fairly stout overall grade generates a pretty fast descent in places as well.

Climb Stats:

Total Elevation - 3,795 ft	**Length - 13.2 miles**
Average Grade - 5.5% (9%)	**Time - 60-100 minutes**

Directions - From the junction of Routes 89 and 31 in the small town of Fairview, head west on 31 to begin the climb.

6%

Southern Utah

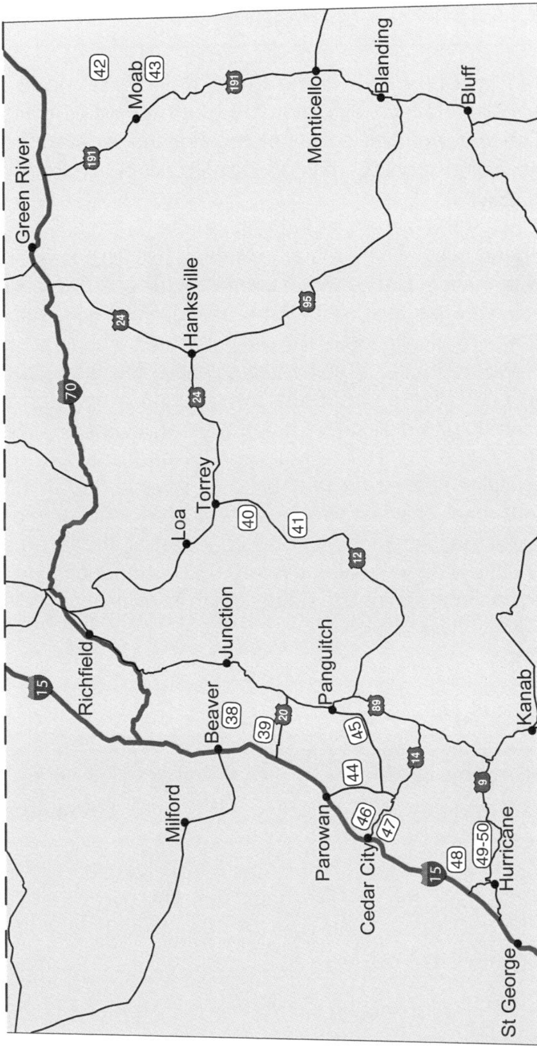

153/Eagle Point

Category 1

The road up Route 153 to the Eagle Point Ski Area is a big mountain climb to high altitude in the south central portion of the state. The route contains sections of solid grade, a descent, along with true alpine scenery. It is an isolated hill but well worth the effort to reach it.

You begin this ascent at the golf course over shallow grade as you head east. Soon you are climbing beside a swift flowing creek with trees in places within a canyon. After a few miles you pull away from the creek through scenic switchbacks that carry more stout grade. On top of the switchbacks the high mountains appear and you enter a small valley where the grade flattens. After several miles of more shallow climbing a right hand turn introduces double digit grade along with big pines and aspens. Soon the Eagle Point Ski Area appears as the slope lessens and the alpine scenery increases. Just beyond, turn left on an unmarked road. This last stretch is steep (contains some double digit grade), passes a few homes and a part of the ski area and dead ends at a parking lot at over 10,000 feet of elevation. You can also continue straight on Route 153 to its own summit (10,000 ft sign) in just over a mile.

Climb Stats:

Total elevation - 4,266 ft	**Length - 17.8 miles**
Average Grade - 4.5% (12%)	**Time - 75-125 minutes**

Directions - From Main Street in Beaver, UT head east on Route 153 for 2.2 miles. You will have just made a 90 degree turn to the left and a golf course is on your left. The climb begins here by continuing east up the hill.

SUMMIT
10,000 FT.

Fremont Pass West

Category 2

The west side of Fremont Pass begins in an isolated and scenic setting as you pull away from Interstate 15. It is a mostly shallow climb that travels through a gap in a ridge of mountains just east of the interstate towards a high altitude ranching valley and eventually several national parks further east and south. There is pleasant scenery along the way and mostly light and intermittent traffic.

You ride over shallow grade to begin the climb away from the interstate. The slope gradually increases as you ride directly east. Several miles in there are two lanes uphill for a bit more room. Soon the grade increases to quite solid which lasts for several miles. Eventually the road decreases back to a single lane as a descent appears. This takes you down into another smaller valley where shallow climbing soon resumes with gradually increasing slope. After another ~1.5 miles the 2nd lane uphill reappears along with more solid grade as you pull out of the scenic and isolated setting. The road gets a bit twisty here and may be the most challenging section of the hill. The climb soon comes to an end at the signed summit. The east side of Fremont Pass is a similar and more shallow ascent (10.3 miles at 2.7% average grade) that begins from Route 89.

Climb Stats:

Total elevation - 1,996 ft	**Length - 10.0 miles**
Average Grade - 3.8% (8%)	**Time - 45-75 minutes**

Directions - On Interstate 15 in isolated Parowan, UT, head north for ~16 miles to Route 20. Turn right here and travel east on 20 for 0.1 miles to begin the listed climb by continuing east up the hill.

SHARP CURVES
STEEP GRADES
NEXT 1 MILE

Boulder Mountain North

Category 2

The north side of Boulder Mountain is a long and somewhat shallow climb just south of Capital Reef National Park in the central portion of the state. Don't let its average grade fool you however as the hill contains stretches of double digit grade along its route. Overall the pedaling is quite variable with a few flats and descents thrown in. One of its most impressive features is the mountain scenery and long views of the surrounding countryside you will see in places as you ascend.

From the climb start the first mile is pretty tame. You enter the national forest at this point and cross a cattleguard to find increased grade. Quickly the pedaling picks up to quite stout as the first of several more challenging ramps is encountered as you ride through a large pine forest with flat topped Boulder Mountain looming to the right in places. Soon the grade eases for a stretch but quickly another stout ramp appears. A flat/descent is then encountered followed by the steepest sustained climbing on the hill as you continue to ride south. Towards the top the grade eases and you find several more flats/descents along with aspen trees and very good high mountain views in places. The listed ascent ends at the signed summit at well over 9,000 feet of elevation.

Climb Stats:

Total elevation - 2,773 ft | **Length - 16.0 miles**

Average Grade - 3.3% (11%) | **Time - 60-100 minutes**

Directions - In Torrey, UT at the junction of Routes 12 and 24, head south on 12 for 6.5 miles to begin the climb at a right hand turn just beyond the junction with Center Street by continuing south on Route 12.

Boulder Mountain South

Category 1

The south side Boulder Mountain is a challenging ascent through some of the best scenery that Utah has to offer. It begins at high altitude and within desert sandstone splendor and ends among aspens within an alpine environment. The grade is solid in places but you will not encounter particularly steep pedaling on this hill. The Tour of Utah visited its scenic slopes in the 2012 event and the road made quite an impression on the race and its professional riders.

You begin the hill climb over fairly solid grade among large pine trees, riding north in isolated surroundings and with sparse traffic. Soon the road swings to the right as the slope picks up a bit. Within several miles you pass the 8,000 foot elevation sign on the right. Just beyond you enter a large meadow with scenic aspen trees and decreasing grade along with amazing views of the Escalante River drainage far below to your right. Eventually you encounter a somewhat long descent which lowers the average grade of this hill significantly. After just over a mile of descending terrain, climbing resumes through an alpine meadow over solid and then decreased grade as you approach the summit. Towards the very top are more very good high mountain views and the ascent ends soon after at the signed summit at well over 9,000 feet of elevation.

Climb Stats:

Total elevation - 2,472 ft **Length - 8.9 miles**

Average Grade - 5.3% (8%) **Time - 45-90 minutes**

Directions - From the 90 degree turn on Route 12 in tiny Boulder, UT head north on 12 for 5.5 very shallow miles to begin the listed climb by continuing north.

SUMMIT
9600 FT.

Castle Valley

Category 1

One of the most difficult ascents in the state, the route begins at the Colorado River near Castle Valley along one of the truly spectacular roads in the United States. Don't let the scenery fool you however as it is a category 1 rated hill. Views of sandstone buttes left and right and sharp mountain peaks straight ahead will certainly keep your attention on this hill. Castle Valley is exposed over its length so it can be quite hot in summer.

As you pull away from the river you are met first by a shallow grade and then a short descent. Climbing quickly resumes and the road turns straight towards the east as the grade gradually steepens. Eventually a few trees appear in the desert wilderness. After 10.6 miles turn right on La Sal Mountain Road. Here the grade increases and quickly you run into your first taste of double digit slope. The road begins to twist through multiple curves as you continue to gain altitude. This section is more narrow and has an alpine feel. After several stout miles the grade eases as you pass through a saddle. Shallow grade lasts for over a mile (long views right) until more solid slope arrives as you ride through an aspen grove. The grade soon eases up to the listed top at the Kokopeli Trailhead on the right (upper section closed in Winter - Manti La Sal National Forest 435 637-2817).

Climb Stats:

Total elevation - 4,255 ft | **Length - 16.8 miles**

Average Grade - 4.8% (12%) | **Time - 75-120 minutes**

Directions - In Moab, UT at the junction of Routes 191 and 128, head north on scenic 128 for 15.2 miles to the road to Castle Valley on the right where the climb begins.

The Big Nasty

Category 1

The climb of Big Nasty is the southern approach to Castle Valley that begins near Moab. It is a true category 1 climb so be prepared before you tackle this one. The road takes riders from desert terrain into high alpine scenery. The grade is quite variable with flats interspersed among more solid ramps including some double digit grade.

You begin over somewhat shallow grade as you pull out of the Moab Valley with sharp peaks directly ahead of you. After several miles the road swings to the left over increased slope. Several miles further a left hand turn introduces the steepest sustained climbing on the hill as the road heads along a ridgeline. A right hand switchback eventually follows with a grade ease and the road soon becomes quite twisty as you continue to gain altitude. Variable slope is present throughout this section and the climb soon ends at an unmarked top (road goes flat at this point and then descends). After a descent the road resumes shallow climbing intermittently but true ascending has ended. It also links up with the previous climb (Castle Valley). The scenery up top is quite good and some make a loop ride by descending that road and then using spectacular but narrow Utah 128 along the Colorado River to get back to Moab.

Climb Stats:

Total elevation - 3,115 ft	**Length - 11.8 miles**
Average Grade - 5.0% (12%)	**Time - 45-75 minutes**

Directions - From Moab, UT head southeast on Spanish Valley Road for a distance to Old Airport Road on the right where the climb begins by continuing straight on Spanish Valley Road.

143 North

Category 1

The north side of Route 143 is isolated but well worth the effort to get there. Keep in mind it is a big hill climb and likely the most difficult in southern Utah. It takes riders through a broad drainage as you head south from the outskirts of Parowan along a shallow grade and ends at very high altitude among the aspens. Along the way you will encounter double digit grade and the mountain town of Brian Head.

The first miles are along a slowly increasing grade and with fairly straight routing within a scenic canyon. As you ride south, the road eventually works its way up to stout slope as it begins to have to twist like a snake in order to ascend the rocky in places canyon. The roadway touches 12% grade more than once along this section. A steep stretch through tight hairpin turns then breaks up the rhythm of the ascent as it abruptly carries you further up the mountain. On top of the S curve the grade then eases but not by much and at mile 11 you pass through the small town of Brian Head to find a bit of congestion and continued stout grade. Leaving the town behind, the grade increases again as you ride along a ridge before easing just before the signed and scenic summit within an alpine setting well above 10,000 feet.

Climb Stats:

Total elevation - 4,339 ft	**Length - 13.9 miles**
Average Grade - 5.9% (12%)	**Time - 75-120 minutes**

Directions - From Interstate 15 the town of in Parowan head south on Route 143. The climb begins at the southern edge of town at the corner of Route 143 and City View Drive by continuing south on 143.

13%
NEXT
10 MILES

143 East

Category 2

The east side of Route 143 from the town of Panguitch is a very long and mostly shallow ascent that ends up in Cedar Breaks National Monument. The route takes you to high altitude with light traffic and there are nice views in places along the way. Never steep, the grade goes up and down on this one. While shallow overall, keep in mind this is a very long climb with some solid ramps on the route so do not underestimate the effort it will take to reach the summit.

To begin you leave the outskirts of Panguitch over solid grade which fairly quickly turns shallow as you ride west. Soon you enter a canyon as the roadway follows a drainage uphill. Eventually riders break out into a series of scenic valleys and trees appear as the grade rolls up and down. After ~15 miles of climbing you pass Panguitch Lake. There are 2 miles of more solid grade some miles above the lake and then the slope returns to more shallow climbing. Towards the top you will ride through alpine meadows with groups of aspens trees adding to the scenery. Just before the end of the ascent you enter Cedar Breaks National Monument and the climb ends soon after at the junction with Route 148 (to the left; Route 143 continues to the right) at well over 10,000 feet of elevation.

Climb Stats:

Total elevation - 3,895 ft	**Length - 30.9 miles**
Average Grade - 2.4% (8%)	**Time - 90-150 minutes**

Directions - In Panguitch, UT, from the junction of Routes 143 and 89, head east on 143 for a short distance (grade change) to begin the climb by continuing east on 143.

40
M.P.H.

Cedar Canyon

Category 1

Cedar Canyon is a long, very scenic and steady grade climb that follows a large drainage from Cedar City up towards Cedar Breaks National Monument over Route 14. The hill takes you just north of Zion National Park into high altitude country and there are good views in places along the way. The riders of the Tour of Utah are aware of this one which was used to open up the 2013 event.

The ascent begins over shallow grade as you leave Cedar City and soon enters a canyon. The route then begins to twist a bit and the grade tends to increase the further east you ride. Eventually the canyon narrows as the slope increases with big rock walls looming over you in places. A bit further along you leave the drainage via a large S curve which carries you higher up the mountain over solid grade which continues for a distance. The grade then eases over the last few miles but offers excellent views of the back side of Zion National Park as you near the top. The climb ends at unmarked (as of 2013) Midway Summit (9,896 feet). Its descent is a nice one due to mostly gentle curves but keep in mind the road is narrow in places and carries some traffic at times.

Climb Stats:

Total elevation - 3,904 ft | **Length - 16.6 miles**

Average Grade - 4.5% (8%) | **Time - 70-120 minutes**

Directions - From Interstate 15 in Cedar City, UT head east on Route 14. Near the east edge of town and just before Highland Road there is a bridge over a creek where the listed climb begins by continuing east on 14.

4-8%
NEXT 10 MI

Right Hand Canyon

Category 1

Right Hand Canyon is another big climb in the southern part of the state that shares its start with Cedar Canyon (previous ascent). It has a different feel however in that it is mostly ridgeline climbing with less vehicle traffic along with long views down onto the Interstate 15 corridor near its top. Use the identical start to bag both of these ascents if you can.

From Cedar City and after 4.4 mostly shallow grade miles on scenic Route 14, turn right on Right Hand Canyon Road (not always marked) to continue. This road quickly swings back in the opposite direction as that of Route 14 and initially twists up the hill over moderate and mostly steady grade. You will eventually head up the mountain along a ridge over solid grade through several switchbacks which ultimately produce excellent views to the west in places. Soon turning to the south, the road then flattens along a ridgeline for a short distance before crossing a cattleguard and resuming climbing, revealing a neighborhood of hillside homes in the distance. The road then heads uphill again through a big S curve over shallow and then moderate slope and eventually into large stands of aspen trees. There are no surprises from this point and the listed climb then eases as it reaches a gap, ending soon after in a wooded setting just before the pavement turns to dirt.

Climb Stats:

Total elevation - 3,228 ft | **Length - 12.1 miles**
Average Grade - 5.1% (8%) | **Time - 60-100 minutes**

Directions - See the Cedar Canyon climb (previous) for directions.

15
M.P.H.

Kolob Canyon

Category 3

The climb of Kolob Canyon, while not a difficult ascent, is one of the most scenic not only in Utah but the entire United States. It carries riders into the dramatic Kolob Canyons section of Zion National Park. While this section of the park is less visited compared to the main portion, you still may have a little traffic to accompany you up the hill but the scenery encountered along the way should be able to get you to its summit. The route is over moderate grade for most of its length and is just long enough to supply a good workout.

You begin over solid grade and a red colored road which matches the exquisite sandstone you will soon encounter. The road swings to the left soon as you pull away from the Visitors Center and Interstate 15. The grade gradually increases as you eventually turn to the east and giant monuments come into view. Pedaling then eases as you pass Taylor Canyon Trailhead. From this point the slope increases and then eases and the road gets a bit twisty as you swing towards the south. The giant ramparts to your left will hold your attention however. A fairly short descent is then encountered before climbing resumes over solid grade. This holds over the final segment up to a small parking lot where the route deadends.

Climb Stats:

Total elevation - 1,163 ft	**Length - 5.2 miles**
Average Grade - 4.2% (8%)	**Time - 20-40 minutes**

Directions - On Interstate 15 in Washington, UT head north for ~30 miles to Exit 49. Turn right (head east) and the climb begins at this junction by continuing east up the hill into Zion National Park.

Kolob Reservoir Road

Category 1

Kolob Reservoir Road is a very scenic and difficult category 1 climb that leads into spectacular Zion National Park along a variable grade in southern Utah. Over a bit more shallow slope on its lower section, the scenery around you is the real attraction on this very big hill. Variably steady grade then greets you along with views of multiple sandstone monuments as you wind up a large drainage.

Beginning at North Creek, ride generally north to northeast over shallow and then moderate slope to begin. In desert terrain here, the road eventually twists through some ranchland along the way. Closer to the top you encounter a tight right hand turn and a short section of steeper grade. The slope then eases and a few more trees appear with the increasing altitude. The climb continues beyond Wildcat Canyon trailhead on the right (gateway to superb canyon hiking and canyoneering) and eventually ends within a scenic aspen grove (always a pleasant sight in the desert) at an unmarked finish at mile 14.9. The paved road continues but while scenic, is without any additional significant climbing and eventually turns to dirt. This is truly an outstanding climb and ride.

Climb Stats:

Total elevation - 4,150 ft | **Length - 14.9 miles**

Average Grade - 5.3% (10%) | **Time - 75-120 minutes**

Directions - The climb begins by getting to the junction of Route 9 and Kolob Reservoir Road in the small town of Virgin, UT. Head up Kolob Reservoir Road for 4.4 miles to the bridge over North Creek where the climb begins.

Zion National Park

Category 4

The climb within the main unit of Zion National Park is perhaps the most scenic in Utah. While not a difficult ascent, it does carry a fairly solid and mostly steady grade along its route as well as a short descent. The road sweeps you uphill through multiple switchbacks (this climb is essentially one switchback after another) and you will likely have some traffic accompany you. The scenery is the thing on this one however and will help you up to its unusual summit just before the dramatic tunnel that carries vehicles further east.

From the bridge over the Virgin River, head east over shallow grade and amid dramatic sandstone temples to begin. Soon you find the first of many turns as you swing to the right to cross the Pine Creek drainage. Quickly you encounter a turn back to the left. This pattern continues as you alternate between riding east and west over moderate slope, gradually gaining altitude up the drainage with giant walls of rock looming over you. As you ascend, pinion pines appear which adds to your viewing pleasure. Towards the top ride east one more time over easing slope with a high wall to your right. The climb ends just before you enter the long tunnel (bikes not allowed) blasted from the orange and brown rock that carries Route 9 traffic into the eastern section of the park.

Climb Stats:

Total elevation - 845 ft | **Length - 3.2 miles**
Average Grade - 5.0% (7%) | **Time - 15-35 minutes**

Directions - From Springdale, UT head north on Route 9 into Zion National Park to the bridge over the Virgin River to begin the climb by continuing east on Route 9.

Other Climbs

Trappers Loop South

Total elevation - 998 ft
Length - 5.3 miles
Average Grade - 3.6% (8%)
Rating - Category 4

The south side of Trappers Loop is a climb over a wide road with some traffic at times. Soon after the start you pass a small neighborhood on the left but beyond are wide open spaces. The grade is stair step up the hill, with solid ramps interspersed with shallow pedaling and the summit is unmarked but obvious.

Directions - In tiny Mountain Green, UT on Interstate 84 east of Ogden, the climb begins at the junction of Old Highway Road and Route 167 by heading north on 167.

Bald Mountain Pass North

Total elevation - 2,255 ft
Length - 16.3 miles
Average Grade - 2.6% (8%)
Rating - Category 2

The north side of Bald Mountain Pass is a shallow and isolated ascent to high altitude. Tree lined, it has a few solid ramps but is mostly shallow climbing. At the very top the scenery is quite alpine and the listed climb ends at the signed summit.

Directions - In Evanston, WY head south on Route 150 for over 10 miles, crossing into Utah. Travel south for another 9 miles, passing the Bear River Ranger Station, to the crossing of the Bear River just beyond to begin the listed climb.

32 West

Total elevation - 1,072 ft | **Length - 4.2 miles**
Average Grade - 4.8% (10%) | **Rating - Category 3**

The west side of Route 32 is a short and interesting climb that takes riders from the Heber City/Midway area towards bigger climbing to the east. The grade is stout to begin so make sure you are ready early on. Soon nice views form to your left as the grade eases a bit. It soon eases further for a stretch and then pops back up to more solid before the listed climb ends at a cut through in the rock. This is an exposed climb so it may be hot during summer at times.

Directions - In Midway, UT at the junction of Routes 40 and 32, head east on Route 32 to begin the listed climb.

Hobble Creek Right Fork

Total elevation - 1,096 ft | **Length - 7.5 miles**
Average Grade - 2.8% (8%) | **Rating - Category 4**

The right fork of Hobble Creek is a shallow ascent near Provo over a very narrow road. From the junction, tree cover quickly closes in on the already tight road. Eventually you enter the national forest and cross several cattleguards. The grade picks up a bit as you continue to ride east but is never steep on this one. You pass several campgrounds as you near climb end. Towards the very end the road makes a right turn and the hill soon ends as the pavement ends.

Directions - In Springville, UT head east on Canyon Road into Hobble Creek Canyon. Continue east for ~3 miles of shallow climbing to the road junction. Head right to begin the climb.

Fremont Pass East

Total elevation - 1,450 ft	**Length - 10.3 miles**
Average Grade - 2.7% (7%)	**Rating - Category 3**

The east side of Fremont Pass is a shallow and bucolic climb at altitude along Route 20 which carries folks towards Interstate 15. There is intermittent traffic on this one but not enough to ruin the ascent. Over the first half you find stair step climbing, eventually through ranch land. There is a nice switchback over increased and stout grade very near climb's end that pulls you out of the valley and the hill ends soon after at the signed summit.

Directions - In Panguitch, UT head north on Route 89 for ~10 miles to its junction with Route 20 (on the left) to begin the climb by heading west on Route 20.

Red Canyon

Total elevation - 1,008 ft	**Length - 4.6 miles**
Average Grade - 4.2% (7%)	**Rating - Category 3**

The east side climb through Red Canyon towards the entrance of Bryce Canyon National Park is a very scenic ascent along with a bit of traffic at times heading to the park. The road immediately gets twisty as you begin. Very soon you are riding through and among the red rocks, the views enchanting in places. Towards the top the grade eases and this one ends far too soon at an unmarked summit on top of the plateau as the grade goes flat.

Directions - From the junction of Routes 89 and 12 just south of Panguitch, UT, head east on Route 12 for a short distance to begin the climb as you enter Red Canyon.

Bryce Canyon West

Total elevation - 1,304 ft **Length - 6.0 miles**

Average Grade - 4.1% (7%) **Rating - Category 3**

The west side climb towards the entrance to Bryce Canyon National Park is a pleasant ascent to altitude. Never steep, it begins in a broad valley. Soon you enter a canyon over increased grade. Pine trees and hoodoos soon appear, giving the climb a Bryce like feel. Towards the top there are two lanes running uphill for a bit more room and the most challenging climbing on the hill. The climb ends as the grade goes flat on top of the plateau.

Directions - In tiny Tropic, UT on Route 12 the climb begins at the west edge of town at the junction of 12 and 550 North (right) by heading west on Route 12.

12 West

Total elevation - 584 ft **Length - 1.7 miles**

Average Grade - 6.5% (13%) **Rating - Category 3**

Used in the 2013 Tour of Utah, the west side of spectacular Route 12 is a very isolated ascent that packs some punch. Quite short, you will find challenging grade in places along its route. After about one mile of moderate grade to begin, the roadway then pops up to quite challenging (double digit) as it twists up a convoluted canyon. After just over another one half mile, the grade eases but remains solid and the climb ends at the signed summit within interesting surroundings.

Directions - In Tropic, UT head east on Route 12 for ~18 rolling miles to begin the listed climb where the grade pops up.

Escalante Canyon East

Total elevation - 1,087 ft | **Length - 4.7 miles**

Average Grade - 4.4% (12%) | **Rating - Category 3**

The east side of Escalante Canyon is an isolated climb through some of the most impressive territory the state of Utah can supply. While its overall grade is not impressive, it does contain a stretch of double digit slope along its route. As you pull away from the river you will ride through amazing walls of sandstone and over moderate grade. Soon the steepest sustained climbing on the hill arrives but does not last long. As you gain altitude the views just get better and you eventually reach a hogback over mostly shallow grade. The listed climb soon ends at an unmarked top with a large pull out on the left side of the road.

Directions - From the bridge over the Escalante River on Route 12 head east to begin the listed climb.

Escalante Canyon West

Total elevation - 1,083 ft | **Length - 5.0 miles**

Average Grade - 4.1% (8%) | **Rating - Category 4**

The west side of Escalante Canyon is an interesting ascent along a narrow and twisty road. From the river you pull away over solid grade to begin. Soon you find a flat and then rolling climbing that takes you into an amazing sandstone bowl. As the road sweeps to the left you find increased grade and views as you gain altitude. The grade then eases after you clear the ridge, there is a cattleguard, and the climb ends soon after at an unmarked top.

Directions - From the bridge over the Escalante River on Route 12 head west to begin the listed climb.

Castle Valley/Gateway

Total elevation - 4,474 ft	Length - 18.9 miles
Average Grade - 4.5% (12%)	Rating - Category 1

Castle Valley/Gateway shares its start with the climb of Castle Valley. Instead of turning right at the junction with La Sal Mountain Road at mile 10.6, keep straight and quickly find a cattleguard and then double digit grade through curves. Soon the pedaling gets easier and long views down into Castle Valley appear. Near the top you encounter another cattleguard as you pass the Fisher Trailhead. Just beyond, the summit is reached as the pavement comes to an end in a scenic setting.

Directions - In Moab, UT head north on Route 128 for just over 15 miles to the road to Castle Valley on the right to begin the listed climb by heading east.

Arches National Park

Total elevation - 506 ft	Length - 1.5 miles
Average Grade - 6.4% (8%)	Rating - Category 4

The climb into Arches is short but packs a punch along with of course spectacular scenery. The road begins to twist up the hill immediately and over solid grade. You may have a few vehicles accompany you through the multiple tight turns but keep turning the pedals. Views are king here and the ascent ends at a saddle as the grade goes flat.

Directions - In Moab, UT head north on Route 191 for several miles to the Arches National Park entrance on the right. Continue north to the tollbooth and the listed climb begins 0.1 miles further north.

Canyonlands National Park

Total elevation - 1,664 ft	**Length - 14.5 miles**
Average Grade - 2.2% (7%)	**Rating - Category 4**

A quite shallow climb overall, Canyonlands is a long and scenic route with a few solid ramps. After a shallow start in a valley the road swings through a big S curve over more solid grade. On top of the bench the grade eases and goes up and down including a few flats and a cattleguard. The listed climb eventually ends at the junction with the road to Deadhorse State Park on the left.

Directions - In Moab, UT head north on Route 191 for ~10 miles to Route 313 (left) where the listed climb begins just beyond the railroad tracks by continuing west on Route 313.

Snow Canyon

Total elevation - 995 ft	**Length - 4.7 miles**
Average Grade - 4.0% (8%)	**Rating - Category 4**

The climb of Snow Canyon, while not a difficult ascent, is quite spectacular as it heads through a rock strewn playground with unique features. It begins over moderate grade as you leave the residences behind. At the state park entrance the grade decreases but views increase as you pass between studded red and white colored walls. Soon the grade increases as you head into the upper valley and its different views of desert rock. Towards the top the slope eases back, the color fades a bit and the listed climb ends just beyond at its junction with Route 18.

Directions - In Ivins, UT northwest of St. George, at the junction of Snow Canyon Parkway and Snow Canyon Drive, head north on Snow Canyon Drive for 0.6 miles to begin the listed climb.

Most Difficult Road Bike Climbs in Utah

1. Guardsman Pass East
2. Powder Mountain
3. 143 North
4. Big Cottonwood Canyon
5. Empire Pass South
6. Little Cottonwood Canyon
7. Kolob Reservoir Road
8. 31 West
9. 153/Eagle Point
10. Castle Valley
11. Castle Valley/Gateway
12. Cedar Canyon
13. Nebo Loop Road North
14. Nebo Loop Road South
15. Alpine Summit East
16. Right Hand Canyon
17. The Big Nasty
18. Alpine Summit West
19. Empire Pass North
20. Monte Cristo Summit West

Most Difficult Road Bike Climbs in Utah

21. 191 South
22. Boulder Mountain South
23. Bald Mountain Pass West
24. North Ogden Divide West
25. Millcreek Canyon
26. Indian Canyon South
27. Wolf Creek Summit West
28. 44 North
29. Bear Lake Summit East
30. Squaw Peak
31. 31 East
32. Wolf Creek Summit East
33. 143 East
34. 191 North
35. Boulder Mountain North
36. 264 East
37. Big Mountain
38. East Canyon
39. Traverse Ridge Road
40. North Ogden Divide East

Most Difficult Road Bike Climbs in Utah

41. Trappers Loop North
42. Fremont Pass West
43. City Creek Canyon
44. Monte Cristo Summit East
45. Bald Mountain Pass North
46. Suncrest Drive
47. Snow Basin Road
48. Bear Lake Summit West
49. Snake Creek Road
50. Bryce Canyon West

Greatest Elevation Gained Climbs

1.	Big Cottonwood Canyon	- 4,814 ft
2.	Nebo Loop Road North	- 4,506 ft
3.	Castle Valley/Gateway	- 4,474 ft
4.	143 North	- 4,339 ft
5.	153/Eagle Point	- 4,266 ft
6.	Castle Valley	- 4,255 ft
7.	Bald Mountain West	- 4,253 ft
8.	Kolob Reservoir Road	- 4,150 ft
9.	Guardsman Pass East	- 3,948 ft
10.	Cedar Canyon	- 3,904 ft

Highest Elevation Attained Climbs

1.	Bald Mountain Pass	- 10,759 ft
2.	143	- 10,573 ft
3.	153/Eagle Point	- 10,342 ft
4.	Cedar Canyon	- 9,814 ft
5.	31	- 9,785 ft
6.	Guardsman Pass	- 9,724 ft
7.	Boulder Mountain	- 9,600 ft
8.	Wolf Creek Summit	- 9,485 ft
9.	264	- 9,413 ft
10.	Nebo Loop Road	- 9,345 ft

Longest Climbs

1. 143 East - 30.9 miles
2. Bear Lake Summit West - 30.5 miles
3. Bald Mountain West - 29.0 miles
4. 31 East - 26.4 miles
5. Nebo Loop Road North - 22.0 miles
6. Castle Valley/Gateway - 18.9 miles
7. Monte Cristo Summit East - 18.2 miles
8. 153/Eagle Point - 17.8 miles
9. Big Cottonwood Canyon - 17.1 miles
10. Castle Valley - 16.8 miles

Steepest Climbs

1. Powder Mountain - 10.0%
2. Ogden Divide North East - 9.4%
3. Ogden Divide North West - 9.3%
4. Guardsman Pass East - 8.6%
5. Empire Pass South - 7.7%
6. Little Cottonwood Canyon - 7.5%
7. Empire Pass North - 7.1%
8. Traverse Ridge Road - 7.1%
9. Squaw Peak - 6.8%
10. 44 North - 6.6%

Fastest Descents

1. Powder Mountain
2. Little Cottonwood Canyon
3. Ogden Divide North West
4. Ogden Divide North East
5. Traverse Ridge Road
6. Snake Creek Road
7. Trappers Loop North
8. Suncrest Drive
9. 143 North
10. Castle Valley

Most Scenic/Spectacular Climbs

1. Zion National Park
2. Alpine Summit East
3. Castle Valley
4. Guardsmans Pass East
5. Powder Mountain
6. Kolob Canyon
7. Snow Canyon
8. Boulder Mountain South
9. Alpine Summit West
10. Little Cottonwood Canyon

15'-9"

Additional Data

The following section contains additional data on the 50 main climbs featured in this guide. They are listed in identical order to their overall listing in the guidebook table of contents. Keys to the 'Traffic' and 'Descent' categories within each climb's additional data section are listed below:

Traffic:

1 – Almost nonexistent traffic
2 – Some intermittent traffic, mostly local
3 – Moderate traffic
4 – Moderate to heavy traffic
5 – Heavy and constant traffic

Descent:

1 – Fast and smooth
2 – Fast with a few obstacles
3 – Speed somewhat blunted by obstacles
4 – Difficult due to road and/or traffic conditions
5 – Danger of bodily harm at almost any speed

Bear Lake Summit East

Total elevation:	1,757 ft	Length:	5.5 mi
Top elevation:	7,822 ft	Average grade:	6.1%
Minimum grade:	2%	Maximum grade:	8%
Distance ≥ 5%:	4.2 miles	Distance ≥ 10%:	0.0 mi
Steepest mile:	6.6%	Steepest 3 miles:	6.3%
Traffic:	3	Descent:	3

Bear Lake Summit West

Total elevation:	3,480 ft	Length:	30.5 mi
Top elevation:	7,822 ft	Average grade:	1.9%
Minimum grade:	0%	Maximum grade:	7%
Distance ≥ 5%:	6.7 miles	Distance ≥ 10%:	0.0 mi
Steepest mile:	5.5%	Steepest 3 miles:	5.1%
Traffic:	3	Descent:	3

North Ogden Divide East

Total elevation:	996 ft	Length:	2.0 mi
Top elevation:	6,191 ft	Average grade:	9.4%
Minimum grade:	4%	Maximum grade:	13%
Distance ≥ 5%:	1.9 miles	Distance ≥ 10%:	1.2 mi
Steepest mile:	10.6%	Steepest 3 miles:	NA
Traffic:	2	Descent:	2

North Ogden Divide West

Total elevation:	1,425 ft	Length:	2.9 mi
Top elevation:	6,191 ft	Average grade:	9.3%
Minimum grade:	4%	Maximum grade:	12%
Distance ≥ 5%:	2.7 miles	Distance ≥ 10%:	1.4 mi
Steepest mile:	10.2%	Steepest 3 miles:	NA
Traffic:	3	Descent:	2

Powder Mountain

Total elevation:	3,179 ft	Length:	6.0 mi
Top elevation:	8,252 ft	Average grade:	10.0%
Minimum grade:	0%	Maximum grade:	17%
Distance ≥ 5%:	5.7 miles	Distance ≥ 10%:	3.6 mi
Steepest mile:	14.4%	Steepest 3 miles:	13.3%
Traffic:	1	Descent:	1

Monte Cristo Summit East

Total elevation:	2,490 ft	Length:	18.5 mi
Top elevation:	8,936 ft	Average grade:	4.1%
Minimum grade:	0%	Maximum grade:	7%
Distance ≥ 5%:	6.6 miles	Distance ≥ 10%:	0.0 mi
Steepest mile:	5.9%	Steepest 3 miles:	5.2%
Traffic:	1	Descent:	3

Monte Cristo Summit West

Total elevation:	3,480 ft	Length:	16.2 mi
Top elevation:	8,952 ft	Average grade:	4.1%
Minimum grade:	0%	Maximum grade:	7%
Distance ≥ 5%:	7.7 miles	Distance ≥ 10%:	0.0 mi
Steepest mile:	5.7%	Steepest 3 miles:	5.3%
Traffic:	2	Descent:	3

Snow Basin Road

Total elevation:	1,627 ft	Length:	7.9 mi
Top elevation:	6,590 ft	Average grade:	3.9%
Minimum grade:	0%	Maximum grade:	8%
Distance ≥ 5%:	4.1 miles	Distance ≥ 10%:	0.0 mi
Steepest mile:	6.6%	Steepest 3 miles:	6.3%
Traffic:	2	Descent:	3

Trappers Loop North

Total elevation:	1,650 ft	Length:	5.8 mi
Top elevation:	6,590 ft	Average grade:	5.4%
Minimum grade:	0%	Maximum grade:	8%
Distance ≥ 5%:	3.9 miles	Distance ≥ 10%:	0.0 mi
Steepest mile:	5.8%	Steepest 3 miles:	5.7%
Traffic:	4	Descent:	2

Bald Mountain West

Total elevation:	4,253 ft	Length:	29.0 mi
Top elevation:	10,759 ft	Average grade:	2.8%
Minimum grade:	0%	Maximum grade:	7%
Distance ≥ 5%:	5.7 miles	Distance ≥ 10%:	0.0 mi
Steepest mile:	5.9%	Steepest 3 miles:	5.8%
Traffic:	3	Descent:	3

Wolf Creek Summit East

Total elevation:	2,330 ft	Length:	10.1 mi
Top elevation:	9,485 ft	Average grade:	4.4%
Minimum grade:	2%	Maximum grade:	8%
Distance ≥ 5%:	4.6 miles	Distance ≥ 10%:	0.0 mi
Steepest mile:	7.3%	Steepest 3 miles:	6.6%
Traffic:	1	Descent:	3

Wolf Creek Summit West

Total elevation:	2,009 ft	Length:	7.3 mi
Top elevation:	9,485 ft	Average grade:	5.2%
Minimum grade:	0%	Maximum grade:	11%
Distance ≥ 5%:	4.7 miles	Distance ≥ 10%:	0.0 mi
Steepest mile:	8.3%	Steepest 3 miles:	8.1%
Traffic:	2	Descent:	3

44 North

Total elevation:	1,627 ft	Length:	4.7 mi
Top elevation:	7,673 ft	Average grade:	6.6%
Minimum grade:	2%	Maximum grade:	9%
Distance ≥ 5%:	3.8 miles	Distance ≥ 10%:	0.0 mi
Steepest mile:	7.1%	Steepest 3 miles:	6.7%
Traffic:	2	Descent:	3

191 North

Total elevation:	1,988 ft	Length:	7.7 mi
Top elevation:	8,063 ft	Average grade:	4.9%
Minimum grade:	0%	Maximum grade:	7%
Distance ≥ 5%:	4.4 miles	Distance ≥ 10%:	0.0 mi
Steepest mile:	6.0%	Steepest 3 miles:	5.3%
Traffic:	2	Descent:	3

191 South

Total elevation:	2,576 ft	Length:	8.9 mi
Top elevation:	8,239 ft	Average grade:	5.5%
Minimum grade:	0%	Maximum grade:	9%
Distance ≥ 5%:	5.6 miles	Distance ≥ 10%:	0.0 mi
Steepest mile:	7.3%	Steepest 3 miles:	6.2%
Traffic:	3	Descent:	3

City Creek Canyon

Total elevation:	1,433 ft	Length:	4.9 mi
Top elevation:	6,122 ft	Average grade:	5.5%
Minimum grade:	0%	Maximum grade:	10%
Distance ≥ 5%:	2.9 miles	Distance ≥ 10%:	0.1 mi
Steepest mile:	7.3%	Steepest 3 miles:	5.7%
Traffic:	1	Descent:	3

Emigration Canyon

Total elevation:	1,311 ft	Length:	7.8 mi
Top elevation:	6,233 ft	Average grade:	3.2%
Minimum grade:	0%	Maximum grade:	8%
Distance ≥ 5%:	2.2 miles	Distance ≥ 10%:	0.0 mi
Steepest mile:	5.9%	Steepest 3 miles:	4.7%
Traffic:	3	Descent:	3

East Canyon

Total elevation:	1,603 ft	Length:	5.4 mi
Top elevation:	7,446 ft	Average grade:	5.6%
Minimum grade:	0%	Maximum grade:	8%
Distance ≥ 5%:	3.2 miles	Distance ≥ 10%:	0.0 mi
Steepest mile:	6.3%	Steepest 3 miles:	5.8%
Traffic:	2	Descent:	3

Big Mountain

Total elevation:	1,881ft	Length:	7.5 mi
Top elevation:	7,446 ft	Average grade:	4.8%
Minimum grade:	0%	Maximum grade:	9%
Distance ≥ 5%:	4.4 miles	Distance ≥ 10%:	0.0 mi
Steepest mile:	7.1%	Steepest 3 miles:	6.9%
Traffic:	2	Descent:	3

Millcreek Canyon

Total elevation:	2,522 ft	Length:	8.8 mi
Top elevation:	7,726 ft	Average grade:	5.4%
Minimum grade:	0%	Maximum grade:	14%
Distance ≥ 5%:	4.7 miles	Distance ≥ 10%:	0.0 mi
Steepest mile:	6.1%	Steepest 3 miles:	5.6%
Traffic:	4	Descent:	3

Big Cottonwood Canyon

Total elevation:	4,814 ft	Length:	17.1 mi
Top elevation:	9,724 ft	Average grade:	5.3%
Minimum grade:	0%	Maximum grade:	12%
Distance ≥ 5%:	9.7 miles	Distance ≥ 10%:	0.1 mi
Steepest mile:	6.6%	Steepest 3 miles:	6.1%
Traffic:	3	Descent:	3

Little Cottonwood Canyon

Total elevation:	3,390 ft	Length:	8.6 mi
Top elevation:	8,755 ft	Average grade:	7.5%
Minimum grade:	3%	Maximum grade:	10%
Distance ≥ 5%:	7.7 miles	Distance ≥ 10%:	0.1 mi
Steepest mile:	9.1%	Steepest 3 miles:	8.4%
Traffic:	3	Descent:	2

Traverse Ridge Road

Total elevation:	1,302 ft	Length:	3.5 mi
Top elevation:	6,129 ft	Average grade:	7.1%
Minimum grade:	0%	Maximum grade:	10%
Distance ≥ 5%:	2.7 miles	Distance ≥ 10%:	0.2 mi
Steepest mile:	8.8%	Steepest 3 miles:	7.3%
Traffic:	5	Descent:	1

Suncrest Drive

Total elevation:	1,167 ft	Length:	3.9 mi
Top elevation:	6,129 ft	Average grade:	5.7%
Minimum grade:	1%	Maximum grade:	9%
Distance ≥ 5%:	2.4 miles	Distance ≥ 10%:	0.0 mi
Steepest mile:	6.6%	Steepest 3 miles:	5.9%
Traffic:	3	Descent:	2

SNOW AVALANCHE AREA
NEXT 2 MILES
NO PARKING OR STOPPING
NOVEMBER 1 - MAY 15

Alpine Summit East

Total elevation:	2,836 ft	Length:	8.7 mi
Top elevation:	8,054 ft	Average grade:	6.2%
Minimum grade:	0%	Maximum grade:	10%
Distance ≥ 5%:	6.5 miles	Distance ≥ 10%:	0.1 mi
Steepest mile:	7.3%	Steepest 3 miles:	6.5%
Traffic:	3	Descent:	3

Alpine Summit West

Total elevation:	2,980 ft	Length:	10.7 mi
Top elevation:	8,054 ft	Average grade:	5.3%
Minimum grade:	0%	Maximum grade:	9%
Distance ≥ 5%:	5.9 miles	Distance ≥ 10%:	0.0 mi
Steepest mile:	6.4%	Steepest 3 miles:	5.9%
Traffic:	3	Descent:	3

Squaw Peak

Total elevation:	1,548ft	Length:	4.3 mi
Top elevation:	6,637 ft	Average grade:	6.8%
Minimum grade:	0%	Maximum grade:	13%
Distance ≥ 5%:	3.6 miles	Distance ≥ 10%:	0.8 mi
Steepest mile:	8.4%	Steepest 3 miles:	6.9%
Traffic:	2	Descent:	3

Guardsman Pass East

Total elevation:	3,948 ft	Length:	8.6 mi
Top elevation:	9,724 ft	Average grade:	8.7%
Minimum grade:	0%	Maximum grade:	18%
Distance ≥ 5%:	7.2 miles	Distance ≥ 10%:	2.1 mi
Steepest mile:	10.3%	Steepest 3 miles:	9.0%
Traffic:	2	Descent:	4

Empire Pass North

Total elevation:	2,094 ft	Length:	5.6 mi
Top elevation:	8,557 ft	Average grade:	7.1%
Minimum grade:	2%	Maximum grade:	12%
Distance ≥ 5%:	4.2 miles	Distance ≥ 10%:	1.0 mi
Steepest mile:	9.8%	Steepest 3 miles:	7.3%
Traffic:	3	Descent:	3

Empire Pass South

Total elevation:	3,181 ft	Length:	7.7 mi
Top elevation:	8,957 ft	Average grade:	7.8%
Minimum grade:	0%	Maximum grade:	18%
Distance ≥ 5%:	5.5 miles	Distance ≥ 10%:	1.4 mi
Steepest mile:	10.3%	Steepest 3 miles:	9.0%
Traffic:	2	Descent:	4

Snake Creek Road

Total elevation:	1,035 ft	Length:	3.3 mi
Top elevation:	6,796 ft	Average grade:	5.9%
Minimum grade:	1%	Maximum grade:	14%
Distance ≥ 5%:	2.7 miles	Distance ≥ 10%:	0.4 mi
Steepest mile:	8.5%	Steepest 3 miles:	6.2%
Traffic:	2	Descent:	2

Nebo Loop Road North

Total elevation:	4,506 ft	Length:	22.0 mi
Top elevation:	8,593 ft	Average grade:	3.9%
Minimum grade:	0%	Maximum grade:	9%
Distance ≥ 5%:	6.6 miles	Distance ≥ 10%:	0.0 mi
Steepest mile:	5.8%	Steepest 3 miles:	5.5%
Traffic:	3	Descent:	3

Nebo Loop Road South

Total elevation:	3,564 ft	Length:	13.8 mi
Top elevation:	9,345 ft	Average grade:	4.9%
Minimum grade:	0%	Maximum grade:	12%
Distance ≥ 5%:	6.7 miles	Distance ≥ 10%:	0.4 mi
Steepest mile:	9.3%	Steepest 3 miles:	8.2%
Traffic:	2	Descent:	3

Indian Canyon South

Total elevation:	3,012 ft	Length:	14.9 mi
Top elevation:	9,114 ft	Average grade:	3.8%
Minimum grade:	0%	Maximum grade:	8%
Distance ≥ 5%:	5.6 miles	Distance ≥ 10%:	0.0 mi
Steepest mile:	7.2%	Steepest 3 miles:	7.1%
Traffic:	2	Descent:	3

264 East

Total elevation:	1,492 ft	Length:	4.8 mi
Top elevation:	9,413 ft	Average grade:	5.9%
Minimum grade:	3%	Maximum grade:	9%
Distance ≥ 5%:	3.7 miles	Distance ≥ 10%:	0.0 mi
Steepest mile:	6.8%	Steepest 3 miles:	6.4%
Traffic:	1	Descent:	3

31 East

Total elevation:	3,685 ft	Length:	26.4 mi
Top elevation:	9,785 ft	Average grade:	2.7%
Minimum grade:	0%	Maximum grade:	7%
Distance ≥ 5%:	6.4 miles	Distance ≥ 10%:	0.0 mi
Steepest mile:	5.5%	Steepest 3 miles:	5.2%
Traffic:	2	Descent:	3

31 West

Total elevation:	3,795ft	Length:	13.2 mi
Top elevation:	9,785 ft	Average grade:	5.5%
Minimum grade:	0%	Maximum grade:	9%
Distance ≥ 5%:	7.5 miles	Distance ≥ 10%:	0.0 mi
Steepest mile:	6.8%	Steepest 3 miles:	6.5%
Traffic:	2	Descent:	3

153/Eagle Point

Total elevation:	4,266 ft	Length:	17.8 mi
Top elevation:	10,342 ft	Average grade:	5.3%
Minimum grade:	0%	Maximum grade:	12%
Distance ≥ 5%:	8.1 miles	Distance ≥ 10%:	0.4 mi
Steepest mile:	9.6%	Steepest 3 miles:	5.8%
Traffic:	2	Descent:	3

Fremont Pass West

Total elevation:	1,996 ft	Length:	10.0 mi
Top elevation:	7,920 ft	Average grade:	3.8%
Minimum grade:	0%	Maximum grade:	7%
Distance ≥ 5%:	4.3 miles	Distance ≥ 10%:	0.0 mi
Steepest mile:	5.7%	Steepest 3 miles:	5.4%
Traffic:	3	Descent:	3

Boulder Mountain North

Total elevation:	2,773ft	Length:	16.0 mi
Top elevation:	9,600 ft	Average grade:	3.3%
Minimum grade:	0%	Maximum grade:	11%
Distance ≥ 5%:	6.3 miles	Distance ≥ 10%:	0.0 mi
Steepest mile:	9.1%	Steepest 3 miles:	7.7%
Traffic:	2	Descent:	3

Boulder Mountain South

Total elevation:	2,472 ft	Length:	8.9 mi
Top elevation:	9,600 ft	Average grade:	5.3%
Minimum grade:	0%	Maximum grade:	8%
Distance ≥ 5%:	4.8 miles	Distance ≥ 10%:	0.0 mi
Steepest mile:	6.2%	Steepest 3 miles:	5.6%
Traffic:	2	Descent:	3

Castle Valley

Total elevation:	4,255 ft	Length:	16.8 mi
Top elevation:	8,327 ft	Average grade:	4.8%
Minimum grade:	0%	Maximum grade:	11%
Distance ≥ 5%:	8.3 miles	Distance ≥ 10%:	0.3 mi
Steepest mile:	8.7%	Steepest 3 miles:	7.2%
Traffic:	1	Descent:	3

The Big Nasty

Total elevation:	3,115 ft	Length:	11.8 mi
Top elevation:	7,946 ft	Average grade:	5.0%
Minimum grade:	0%	Maximum grade:	12%
Distance ≥ 5%:	6.1 miles	Distance ≥ 10%:	0.7 mi
Steepest mile:	9.2%	Steepest 3 miles:	5.5%
Traffic:	1	Descent:	3

143 North

Total elevation:	4,339 ft	Length:	13.9 mi
Top elevation:	10,420 ft	Average grade:	5.9%
Minimum grade:	1%	Maximum grade:	12%
Distance ≥ 5%:	8.6 miles	Distance ≥ 10%:	0.3 mi
Steepest mile:	8.4%	Steepest 3 miles:	7.2%
Traffic:	2	Descent:	3

143 East

Total elevation:	3,895 ft	Length:	30.9 mi
Top elevation:	10,573 ft	Average grade:	2.4%
Minimum grade:	0%	Maximum grade:	8%
Distance ≥ 5%:	6.7 miles	Distance ≥ 10%:	0.0 mi
Steepest mile:	6.5%	Steepest 3 miles:	6.0%
Traffic:	1	Descent:	3

Cedar Canyon

Total elevation:	3,904 ft	Length:	16.6 mi
Top elevation:	9,814 ft	Average grade:	4.5%
Minimum grade:	0%	Maximum grade:	8%
Distance ≥ 5%:	7.5 miles	Distance ≥ 10%:	0.0 mi
Steepest mile:	8.1%	Steepest 3 miles:	5.5%
Traffic:	3	Descent:	3

Right Hand Canyon

Total elevation:	4,339 ft	Length:	12.1 mi
Top elevation:	9,138 ft	Average grade:	5.1%
Minimum grade:	0%	Maximum grade:	8%
Distance ≥ 5%:	6.3 miles	Distance ≥ 10%:	0.0 mi
Steepest mile:	5.7%	Steepest 3 miles:	5.6%
Traffic:	2	Descent:	3

Kolob Canyon

Total elevation:	1,163 ft	Length:	5.2 mi
Top elevation:	6,217 ft	Average grade:	4.2%
Minimum grade:	0%	Maximum grade:	8%
Distance ≥ 5%:	2.3 miles	Distance ≥ 10%:	0.0 mi
Steepest mile:	5.8%	Steepest 3 miles:	4.8%
Traffic:	3	Descent:	3

Kolob Reservoir Road

Total elevation:	4,150 ft	Length:	14.9 mi
Top elevation:	7,965 ft	Average grade:	5.3%
Minimum grade:	0%	Maximum grade:	10%
Distance ≥ 5%:	7.7 miles	Distance ≥ 10%:	0.0 mi
Steepest mile:	6.4%	Steepest 3 miles:	6.1%
Traffic:	2	Descent:	3

Zion National Park

Total elevation:	845 ft	Length:	3.2 mi
Top elevation:	4,849 ft	Average grade:	5.0%
Minimum grade:	0%	Maximum grade:	7%
Distance ≥ 5%:	1.7 miles	Distance ≥ 10%:	0.0 mi
Steepest mile:	5.5%	Steepest 3 miles:	5.2%
Traffic:	5	Descent:	3

Climb Logs

Northern Utah:

Climb	Date
Bear Lake Summit East	
Bear Lake Summit West	
North Ogden Divide East	
North Ogden Divide West	
Powder Mountain	
Monte Cristo Summit East	
Monte Cristo Summit West	
Snow Basin Road	
Trappers Loop North	
Bald Mountain Pass West	
Wolf Creek Summit East	
Wolf Creek Summit West	
44 North	
191 North	
191 South	

Salt Lake City/Provo/Midway:

Climb	Date
City Creek Canyon	
Emigration Canyon	
East Canyon	
Big Mountain	
Millcreek Canyon	
Big Cottonwood Canyon	
Little Cottonwood Canyon	
Traverse Ridge Road	
Suncrest Drive	
Alpine Summit East	
Alpine Summit West	
Squaw Peak	
Guardsman Pass East	
Empire Pass North	
Empire Pass South	
Snake Creek Road	

Central Utah:

Climb	Date
Nebo Loop Road North	
Nebo Loop Road South	
Indian Canyon South	
264 East	
31 East	
31 West	

The top of Wolf Creek Summit

Southern Utah:

Climb	Date
153/Eagle Point	
Fremont Pass West	
Boulder Mountain North	
Boulder Mountain South	
Castle Valley	
The Big Nasty	
143 North	
143 East	
Cedar Canyon	
Right Hand Canyon	
Kolob Canyon	
Kolob Reservoir Road	
Zion National Park	